A Journey of Hearts
Navigating life experiences

Tammy J. Bowers
Edited by Nancy Czarnecki

© 2014 Tammy J. Bowers

All Rights Reserved.

No part of this publication may be reproduced, stored in a retrieval system, or transmitted, in any form or by any means, electronic, mechanical, photocopying, recording, or otherwise, without the written permission of the author.

First published by Dog Ear Publishing
4010 W. 86th Street, Ste H
Indianapolis, IN 46268
www.dogearpublishing.net

ISBN: 978-1-4575-3273-3

Library of Congress Control Number: has been applied for

This book is printed on acid-free paper.

Printed in the United States of America

Acknowledgements
Heart to Heart
by Tammy Bowers

This book was a journey, one I am proud and excited as it come to fruition! It is a beginning of what will be several Inspirational books, a series sharing life experiences on a variety topic and circumstances! I believe each of us has a journey to share, once written how eye-awakening it becomes as it unfolds on paper, creating a greater understanding of who we are, what we have accomplished and how we got where we are today!

Our journey of hearts brings hope and inspiration in helping others and I am honored to call these amazing 1st Edition Authors my extended family; to each of you I give you a hug of gratitude and my "thank you" for your contributions, experiences and expertise in sharing your journey's with us!

My Inspirational Authors: Adele Marie, Drema Bonavitacola, Jeannette Bambarger, Stacey Stirmer, Ellis Woodward, Lynn Molnar, Buddy Teaser, Lisa Shah and
a big thanks to our editor and my friend Nancy Czarnecki

My family is my core, they have inspired and supported me not just in this endeavor but several others ventures over the years, always encouraging me to pursue that which resides in my heart! They will always have my love and gratitude, especially my husband Jeff, who has always allowed me to be me; and my children Sarah, Josh, and Zach; as well as my Mom Joan, my Father-in-Law Stanley, and to all my family and friends, I am so thankful to have you in my life!

I chose the "White Rose" because to me it symbolizes purity of heart, and it's soothing. This particular rose perfectly reflects the openness of these authors, and how open we can be to possibilities! If you look closely, you can see a swirl (of gratitude) from the center outward, watch as it opens clockwise opening up wider and wider- HOPE and Inspiration! If you feel the spark of inspiration and you would like to share, please submit to nutmom3@comcast.net , we might select your journey to be a part of our next Inspirational Series!

"Thank you" from our hearts to yours for your purchase of "A Journey of Hearts"!

Hearts of Inspiration

1. Heart~2~Heart by *Tammy Bowers* 1
2. Right Here, Right Now by *Ellis Woodward* 18
3. A Journey of Love and Honor by *Adele Marie* 35
4. Destiny by *Drema Bonavitacola* 51
5. Full Hands/Full Heart by *Stacey Stirmer* 59
6. Heal You by *Jeanette Bambarger* 74
7. My Animated Life by *Lisa Shah* 89
8. Transformational Love by *Lynn Mohar* 106
9. Happy or Grateful by *Buddy Teaser* 122

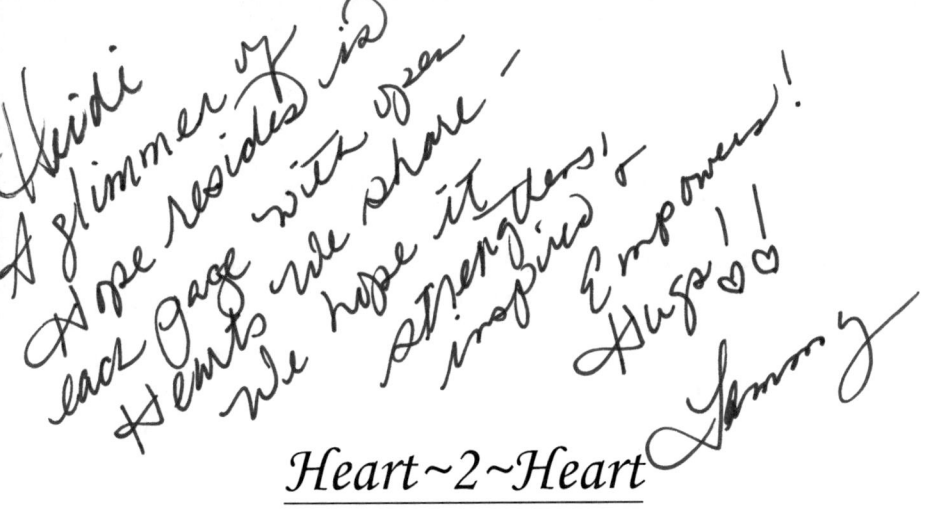

Heart~2~Heart

Our continuous journey as Mother and Daughter by
Tammy Bowers

> "As mothers, we hug, smile, support, multi-task and compartmentalize, using all of ourselves by sharing our heart, mind and spirit; guiding and protecting our children from heartache, always surrounding them with the core of us, which is a Mother's heartfelt LOVE!"
>
> —Tammy Bowers

My journey would start on May 28, 1988, with the birth of our first-born, a daughter Sarah weighing in at 7 lbs 3 ounces. She was beautiful, perfect from head to toe, looking so much like Jeff with lots of dark hair and deep brown eyes. I found myself smiling as I watched Jeff who was beaming with pride holding his little princess, a Dad for the first time!

I had imagined this moment for nine months, bursting with excitement to be a Mom. My heart filled up with an indescribable love that only a mother could best describe, as joyous, with so much happiness at that very moment. It was as if my heart was singing from the inside out. Instinctively, as we all know, change was inevitable and so began the motherly instinct to protect and re-evaluate things of importance, as it is no longer about us, but Sarah. Over time, two boys and a dog name Lexie would all become a part of our family.

Advocating for our children came naturally. I would be their voice until they were strong enough to share on their own and for Sarah that did not take long! It was at that moment, our journey together began, and I recognized that over time we would have similarities and differences; accomplishments and challenges, as well as many wonderful memories together as a family. I smile, as I cherish each step we have taken individually and together, from this moment of birth to present, each experience is one of a memory held close to my heart, lasting forever!

> *"Accept each moment as a gift, to be received with joy"*
> —Dr. Nido Qubein

The winds of change came at our door, our world as we knew it dramatically changed in a split moment, going topsy-turvy. At the age of 19 yrs old, Sarah would be diagnosed with an extremely rare and incurable kidney disease called (LPHS) Loin Pain Hematuria Syndrome! (3,000 worldwide; NIH classified LPHS as an orphan disease - http://rarediseases.info.nih.gov/gard/6920/loin-pain-hematuria-syndrome/more-about-this-disease)

> *"The purpose of a doctor or any human is to increase the person's quality of life."*
>
> *"Death is not the enemy sir, Indifference is! You treat a disease, you win, you lose.*
>
> *You treat a person; I guarantee you'll win, no matter what the outcome."*
> —Patch Adams

I remember and remind myself, "God only gives us as much as we can handle" and by keeping "faith, family and friends" close they will help me through multiple situations.

Life is about choices, discovering chances and making changes. If we only focus on the "what ifs", the negativities, wallowing in self-pity, we will miss opportunities that present themselves to us. I decided to take a deep breath, finding my inner strength along with some "chutzpah", to move forward to do whatever it took to help our baby. I thought the solution would be easy in finding a collaborative medical team, but in reality, it would be challenging, due to the rarity of her illness. I would keep the faith, not give up I would find them, and their willingness to give her 110% of their time, care, compassion and expertise, because only the best would do for our girl!

The reality is some days are difficult, very difficult for her and for us; others are of normalcy. We never know day to day what will be happening physically or emotionally as chronic illness affects the entire body.

Recently, I heard on the radio, "the impossible gives birth to possible" it struck a chord with me. "Don't give up" stay focused to dream the dream of hope and possibilities, no matter what happens. I myself want to keep optimism alive in my heart, but the reality is that it is up to Sarah to stay determined, hopeful and to pull from the strength within her and fight the fight as we are standing right beside her. This life experience has brought us together; finding pieces of ourselves we never realized existed, strength in moving forward, and one day to pay it forward, helping others going through similar situations.

> *"When I let go of what I am, I become what I might be"*
>
> —Lao Tzu

With all the professionals she has seen over the years, not one indicated she needed to see a Nephrologist and that her pain was in the kidney region. Taking the initiative, I began to research and set-up a consultation with Dr. Marc Brazie. Dr. Brazie was a Fellow at University of Maryland –Nephrology Department; he was amazing, persistent, and supportive; determined to find a diagnosis. Establishing a relationship with him right away would have been beneficial as he would be the first on her team to initiate the care. Over the course of several months, Sarah experienced numerous tests, along with a very painful double kidney biopsy; in the end, it would confirm her rare diagnosis of LPHS – Loin Pain Hematuria Syndrome. It would be imperative to have an accurate and second opinion as to this diagnosis, so we took her to see the top specialist Dr. Michael Choi, Chief of Nephrology at Johns Hopkins University; unfortunately, he too would confirm her diagnosis; "I wish there was more I do for her, but presently there are no trials or research and no cure".

We returned to Dr. Brazie and he continued to treat her, then about a year or so later, he offered a rainbow of hope, as there was a researcher in Ohio organizing an experimental trial for LPHS patients. It was a new procedure called a Kidney Radio Frequency Ablation, 10 patients had participated. It was risky with only a 50/50 chance with no guarantees, but with no other options, and we thought it would be worth it. It was a very painful procedure for Sarah, as it burns the nerves surrounding the kidney area, these nerves grow back over time, and the procedure would need to be repeated. I was devastated for her, when unfortunately the procedure did not work, this door may have closed but I needed to believe another would open over time, we both knew it was back to the drawing board.

> *"Family Physicians – cure sometimes, treat often, comfort always!"*
> —*Dr. Kevin Ferentz mantra, a quote from his mentor Dr. James Nunn*

In my opinion, the stars were aligned the day, we were referred to a Family physician named Dr. Kevin Ferentz, working at University of Maryland Family Medicine Department, having 30 years experience, and living up to his reputation as kind and compassionate doctor to all his patients. I feel lucky and comforted in knowing that he is her quarterback, advocating for her and having her back. He is someone she can rely on both physically and emotionally. He mentioned to me "Chronic illness affects the entire family not just the patient", and then offered an open door policy to our entire family. What a welcome breath of fresh air, a GIFT to us that day and he became a welcome part of our family!

> *"Don't walk in front of me. I may not follow, don't walk behind me, I may not lead, Walk beside me and be my friend"*
> —*Mother Theresa*

On December 6, 2012 at 6 AM, our phone rang, Jeff listened intently, as the resident at the hospital explained, "I am so sorry to wake you, but we had a serious situation with your daughter and resuscitation was needed". Without hearing the words, my heart began to race, as he was gathering information, I knew something horrible had happened! Our car ride was a quiet, rehashing of the day, just trying to make sense of it all! Keeping my expression as calm as I could, focusing on the positive; she is alive and breathing! Silently I pray to myself, "God, please continue to help her until we get there!"

Arriving at hospital, we took one glance at each other for reassurance; she was going to be okay! We were greeted by her nurses and Doctor, "Unfortunately, no beds were available in the ICU. But do not worry; we will be watching her very carefully, having a nurse in her room at all times". As they continued to speak, I was in a dream state just walking; I needed to see for myself that she was okay, Jeff and I continued to walk to her room. "She is not out of the woods, she had an extremely low potassium level which as you know is dangerous, and it was a factor in what happened here today". It would take several bags of potassium, until her levels returned to the normal range. As I held and hugged her tightly my grateful tears began flowing, she unleashed her fighting spirit that day, and for me a memory embellished on my heart forever!

> *"A strong positive mental attitude will create more miracles than any wonder drug"*
>
> —*Patricia Neal*

It has not been easy, to say the least- adjustments and sacrifices made over the years. It has been disappointing but it is what happens when a chronic illness settles into your family.

At times I watched in anger at the harshness and lack of education of some of medical professionals who treated her, this behavior was very disheartening. She bared the brunt of attitude and judgment over and over again; it was harsh and horrible and a tough lesson.

My heart would take a leap when she had doctors and nurse who took the time to get to know her, her illness and ask her questions. She became empowered and confident and then discovered if she educated herself, and learned their language; she could teach them about her illness and get better treatment. She created and organized a LPHS patient binder, including documents of importance, those describing her symptoms, copies of her test results, medical allergies, surgeries, and medications. I was so proud of how she took back control of her health care, respect and her dignity!

> *"Hope is the thing with feathers that perches in the soul and sings the tunes without the words and never stops at all"*
>
> —*Emily Dickinson*

I became a mom of interchangeable hats, especially as she became older, as it was more difficult to sit quietly on the sidelines, when she made her own decision. Whether I agreed or disagreed, theses were her decisions to make. I would voice my opinion but the bottom line they were hers to make. I would have my moments of uncontrollable *tears; frustration and anger, as well asking* "WHY?" wishing her situation were different. How do I get through it, honestly, there are times I am not sure accept for relying on faith, family, friends, and having an amazing husband who lends me support when I need it. Jeff's spirit has truly helped all of us over the years with his sense of humor, strength and reassurance, that no matter what, "it is going to be OK"!

As parents this illness has affected both of us, more adjustments as a couple were needed, it was time to re-prioritize just as I did when they were babies, taking back control just as Sarah had done, but one day at a time as a couple once again. We established a "Date night" once a week. It goes without saying, if do not take care of ourselves how could we take care of her, reenergize and clear our minds was the perfect recipe!

I am encouraged by my boys and how they have handled all that their sister has gone through over the years; not always knowing what to say or what to do but their hearts always in the right place in helping her as best they can.

People will laugh when I say I had furry daughter "Lexie" who allowed me to vent to her, release my frustrations, was there to dry my tears on her fur as she listened intently. Giving me an unconditional love, I feel she has been a gift from God, as she arrived just a few years before Sarah's diagnosis and has helped each of us on separate occasions. What a beautiful giving creature, we will never forget her; she became instantly a member of our family!

> *"To laugh often and love much, to appreciate beauty, to find the best in others, to give one's self, this is to have succeeded."*
>
> —*Ralph Waldo Emerson*

February of 2012, we found Sarah collapsed on the floor where she had laid over night. She was breathing, but her leg was extremely swollen. Jeff picked her up and got her from the floor to the bed. She tried to reassure us, "I must have fallen and passed out, but I'll be fine". I proceeded with my routine for the morning, taking Zach to school, but on my way back, I received a call, "Mom something is just not right, I think I need to go to the hospital". It is about a 30-minute drive, by the time I got home, her legs, arms and hands were starting to swell. We left immediately though we were both nervous and became chatty on the way, we are alike in that way, wanting to reassure the other one, that is was going to be Okay! I observed the swelling increasing to both legs. Once we arrived, they took her right back. After testing she was diagnosis with rhabdomilosis* a very serious medical condition, due a reaction from a medication, which had her collapsing on the floor for numerous hours. Hospitalized for about a week it reminded me once again, how tough she is fighting the fight and Winning! (*Rhabdomyolysis (rhabdo=skeleton +myo=muscle + lysis=breakdown) is a condition in which muscles break down quickly and spill their contents into the blood stream. Myoglobin is a protein that is contained in muscle cells, and if enough is spilled into the blood stream, it can clog the kidney's filtering system and lead to kidney failure and a variety of other serious medical http://www.medicinenet.com.)

> *"With a new day comes, new strength and new thoughts"*
> —Eleanor Roosevelt

Traveling together on this journey has taught us both about hospitals, their efficiencies, key functionality, protocol, as well as the need for flexibility and patient advocacy. It is a vital role. I understand the importance as Sarah's caregiver and advocate. Most hospitals are overcrowded and understaffed, but they still need to have eye and ears around to help them be accountable for care of family members. Over the years Sarah has had numerous reactions to medications, and by my observations I could relay any information she was unable to the professionals to take good care of her. There were times she was unable to talk or walk and retrieval or processing words could be challenging! For me I found that by building a relationship with nurses that would also lend a hand in care, that when I was unable to, they would be there advocating for her. I give them a lot of credit, having such big hearts. They are her medical angels by trade, and I am always so grateful for the care she receives by them. I would be sure to give them even a small gift a token of my appreciation; they gifted me on many occasions with hugs, and kindness to my family. Sarah herself would share with me her experiences when so many would take time to sit on her bedside, engaging in a conversation, giving her comfort, trust and reassurance. These are such simple but treasured heartfelt gestures, that only time is given and the heart of communication!

> *"Gratitude is not the only greatest of virtues, but the parent of all others"*
> —Marcus Cicero

About a year and half ago on a Friday, we had another trip to the hospital, arriving at five AM to the ER with abdominal pain. The resident took charge, gave her some fluids along with some pain medication and after some time, he offered her a medication, which he thought would help her through the weekend. She hesitated, mentioning, she has had numerous serious reactions to medication. He reassured her by taking the medication she would feel better by Saturday, go home rest, continue with fluids and return on Monday for her procedure. She was reluctant but swallowed the pill, she again reminded him of her numerous reactions to medication, his response was "it's a benign pill, you will be fine". He provided her with a prescription for weekend and asked me to get the car to meet her at the ER entrance; present time was five PM, Rush Hour.

My motherly instinct told me something was not right especially as I saw her pale pasty coloring and she was having trouble walking, in the pit of my stomach I was thinking that she really should not be leaving. I greeted her with a smile at the ER door, getting her into the car, and responded, "Let's just get you home you will feel better once you are in your own bed". It was less than fifteen minutes from hospital and the struggle began with breathing; she is trying to scream out, "Call 911". Over the years even when it was bad, she has never asked me to call 911, I knew it was bad. As scared as I was, I spoke the dispatcher on the phone, asking me a variety of questions about Sarah, but as I looked over at her Sarah was fading fast, I said, and "Please Hurry"!

The fire trucks and paramedics arrive; I greeted them, explaining the situation as best I can, but also in the corner of my eye witnessing how the woman paramedic was treating Sarah. She was unwilling to help her out of the car; I am thinking to myself, I just want them to take her to the hospital immediately. I can see the distress in Sarah's face; the woman firefighter would not touch Sarah and asked that she get herself out of the car. I was mortified, "what" I am thinking to myself, they did not help her and asked her to walk on her own into the ambulance as unsteady as she was, she got in. I was so upset at this point not understanding this type of protocol. Sarah tried to talk to them but was unable and the woman thought Sarah was not cooperating. They asked me again about the medication she took, I said, "the hospital gave her a medication; she had never had before, if you call them they can tell you" knowing they direct line of communication to the hospital. I called Dr. Ferentz without hesitating he said, "Take her immediately back to University". She made it to the ambulance, I hugged them and said, "Thank you" finally they were on their way. I called Jeff, we met at the hospital and by the time we got there, things were underway. Later I would find out about the treatment or lack thereof in the ambulance on the way back to the ER. I am still mortified; an experience and education I will remember for quite some time!

This was, of course, a major life threatening reaction to the medication given in the ER, which traumatized her body, shutting down her organs one by one, including her speech. In the ambulance, days later she told me, "I could hear them but could not speak" and her body thrashed and convulsed inside the ambulance. The paramedics had not covered her up or secured her to the bed, by the time, she returned to hospital she was covered in vomit and other bodily fluid, and she was crashing-dying!

Jeff and I arrived at Hospital and I recognized the resident who had treated her. He said, "Oh did you forget something", and I said, "My daughter was brought back by ambulance, I believe she had a major reaction to the medicine you gave her". He quickly jumped up out of his chair, his face pale, and raced over to where everyone was taking care of her. We could see my baby girl on the bed, her body seizing, jolting, projectile vomiting, with body fluid going and her body flaring. It was as if we were watching a movie, a nightmare this was not happening our daughter. "Why did that doctor not believe my daughter, especially when she tried to tell him? She knew her body!"

Several Shock trauma doctors and an ER team of medical professionals were taking care of her, they did speak to us, but it was quite overwhelming. We were listening but not really hearing, "The next 24 hours are critical, she may not make it" I was in shock and praying to myself. Both Jeff and I were holding hands, and I am sure he was saying, as was I, "This was the absolute WORST day of my life!"

They finally allowed us to be in the room, it was as if I was in a movie, I held her hand and whispered as I watched her eyes roll back inside her head, "Sarah, we are here with you, please stay with us, you've got to fight, WE LOVE YOU!" I repeated it over and over again, hoping by our words it would reach down she could hear me to give her the strength she needed to fight, as I knew this would be a major fight, but one she would survive once again!

She was unable to speak until Sunday, and when she spoke, my anger would intensify and a "roar" that would be felt by the Chief of the County Fire Department. I felt as though she had been violated medically with a lack of respect as a patient, the details are for her to share, but the treatment they gave my baby was horrifying. After her hospitalization, once she returned home, she scheduled a meeting with the Deputy Fire Chief. He came to our home, to meet with Sarah and discuss in person what transpired that day. She was so courageous to me, as well as brave, having to relive every detail of that day, and the horrific experience all over again. As tough as it was, she said "what if it was someone who was unable to speak, they may be deaf, or disabled, elderly or otherwise compromised, what they did to me yes it was cruel, disrespectful and unwarranted. I do not want anyone to be treated in that manner ever!" I was so very proud of her that day!

> *"I cannot change the direction of the wind, but I can adjust my sails to reach my destination."*
>
> — *Jimmy Dean*

Fear is one of those nasty words, admittedly, it comes and goes, but if we come to grips with the worst fear possible sometimes it is easier to swallow, for me three times almost losing my daughter, this is my fear and one I hope number four will never follow. I believe in empathy, compassion, kindness, positivity's, love, laughter and joy, fear is not one I want to hang on to for any reason but it's there it lingers and hangs around whether we like it or not.

Through this experience with Sarah, I have witnessed the body languages of doctors and residents-the lack of eye-to-eye contact, which again is a lack of respect to patients and their families. I have often said "shame on them" for not getting to know or understand. Shame on them for persevering without truly knowing all the ins and outs of LPHS. All patients deserve respect, truth and trust by their doctors and medical staff; just recently, I had an experience where a 3rd year Resident would rather look at the floor while explaining my daughter's situation. Once I reminded him to look me in the eye, as he was talking to me, he apologized.

Most doctors and medical staff, I have admired and appreciated, but it is an eye opener for those that do not adhere to the same values as care and compassion. Doctor's unwritten bylaws are to have respect. Patients will see it in their eyes, for the eyes are the windows to our souls. For those few bad apples in the bunch, addressing a patient with arms folded at the foot of the bed, cell phone in hand along with notebook, looking at their notes never once looking up at the patient, completely unaware of patients emotions, fear or condition is shameful. I hope that doctors such as the Dr. Ferentz's, Dr. Brazie's, Dr. Choi's and Dr. Schwartz's of the world can make these changes for other individuals, by mentoring, explaining the importance of genuine empathy and sincerity as well as respect that goes hand in hand with education and experience for patients and their families.. I have witnessed how by the little act of kindness, the gift of giving, over time lends a hand in healing and reassuring physically and from the heart.

> *"If you don't like something, change it; if you can't change it change your attitude"*
>
> —*Maya Angelou*

After her last episode, her illness became more complex, and it began to wreak havoc in other areas of her body, especially her colon. Joining our team was Dr. Jeffrey Schwartz, from Maryland General. Over time, she would have numerous procedures and become very familiar with 4th Floor GI nurses and anesthesiologist at Maryland General. On April 4, 2014, she had four procedures in one day, and a lot of respect and love given to her that day. It began with what seemed like a revolving door of heartfelt emotions shared by her GI medical professionals, each of them taking time out of their busy day to visit with her. This was a first for me, an extremely rare occurrence, and something I feel privileged to have experience with her! They shared their observations of what they saw in her, reminding Sarah and us what an amazing girl she had become, how much she has taught herself medical terminology and educated others about her illness. It is because of her knowledge and strength that doors will be opened. Her eyes lit-up and my heart beamed with pride, as these medical angels bestowed on her that day an offering that, once she had completed her nursing or medical training, they were eager for her to be a part of their team. Wow, she had HOPE and opportunity awaiting her, what a special gift they gave to her and without their realizing it, a gift to me and our family!

> *"Character cannot be developed in ease and quite, only through experiences of trial and suffering can the soul be strengthened, vision cleared, ambition, inspired and success achieved."*
>
> —*Helen Keller*

"NO CURE, NO OPTIONS"; those words just do not exist for me. I became vigilant and empowered, acknowledging that education and awareness are the keys to unlocking some connections and resources. With the help of family, friends and some medical professionals as well networkers, I coordinated a successful fundraiser event at the Engineers Club in Baltimore. I wanted to create the awareness factor, helping not only Sarah but also those suffering with LPHS globally. Our website provided a platform of hope and reassurance that she was not in it alone, lending a hand in offering a support system, shared information, and treatments. "You never know who knows someone", and I will never give up HOPE, transferring my feelings of helplessness to something stronger- empowerment for both of us, building bridges globally to other families dealing with this horrible illness suffering with LPHS. Finding the strength in advocacy has created a united front a bond of a Mother's love for her daughter that "NO Cure" would have no place here!

"Never, never, never give up! "

—*Winston Churchill*

Do I wish things were different absolutely! Should I wallow in self-pity or, stay the course with encouragement? Education will open that closed door to possibilities. I hope in this lifetime that more medical professionals will also open their eyes to alternative treatments encompassing the mind body and spirit of the patients. If I could offer any advice to you, I would say advocating for yourself and for family, also journaling is an incredible tool, to release excess energy both good and bad, putting it down on paper; sometimes I even burn it to help release my emotions.

Faith, either going to Church or Synagogue with my family offers me time that I may not take, time of reflection, to gain a greater understanding and acceptance using spirituality as a strong foundation. Or even just time, to have a quite meditation at home by lighting a candle with quiet music quiets my mind and gives me a sense of peace. . Jeff will joke, on the days he can see it was not such a great day, "Ok, Momma its time you get some Zen on!" One or more of these make my heart sing and he is aware of how much they have helped me!

As I mentioned before, take time individually, as a couple, or as mother and daughter, with whomever is going through the chronic illness and let them focus on something other than the medical. A walk, exercise, dinner, coffee, or just being together truly helps raise my endorphins and I can only imagine it helps the patient. A wise man (my dad) once told me *"Things happen for a reason, we may not know why at the time, but having faith and belief that in time it will all work out!"* It was tough in the beginning to accept the things I cannot change. I have learned alongside Sarah on this journey we have traveled together. I found we have illuminated our inner strength, empowered each other, leaned on each other, supported each other, and made a connection as mother and daughter. It is one of nurturing and respect, our hearts beat separately but also together. We will always be hoping for a cure, a better life for her; moving forward to continue to help her with our heart-2-heart connection, in time passing it forward helping others in similar situations!

"No bird soars too high if he soars with his own wings"

—*William Blake*

Right Here, Right Now
by Ellis Woodward

"You've got to Ac-Cen-Tchu-Ate the Positive..."

On Thanksgiving eve, November 27, 2013, I sat on the edge of the bed to which my mother has been largely consigned for the last seven months, and the two of us sang, "Three Little Fishies In A Little Bitty Pool," "Save The Bones For Henry Jones," and "Accentuate The Positive". That we sang these particular up-and off-beat songs together was profound and significant only because, on that day, my mom was eight and a half years into her Alzheimer's diagnosis, and most other commonplace expressions of awareness and cognitive strength had long since vanished from her life. Included in her lost abilities were, to a very large degree, the ability to speak coherently or formulate language into any kind of intelligible sentence. For the most part, other than some predictable, parroted-echo responses, most of her attempts at speech have become indecipherable, even as regards their intent – often, we can figure out what people are saying because we are able to understand what they are *trying to say*, as is often the case with small children. With my mom, however, that intent is no longer discoverable, most of the time. And yet, there we were, singing some rather complex lyrics and melodies together, with my mom's surprisingly strong voice, not only chiming in or mimicking, but adding appropriate (and accurate) harmony parts and rhythmic syncopations. I was surprised and tickled, grinning all over myself at my amazing good fortune to be there and drink in yet another moment of unimaginable, unadulterated pleasure in my mother's remarkable, durable presence. It was a gift moment, for certain, but the kind of gift that one must be ready - and able - to receive. It was the gift of joy, wrapped in a moment, a freestanding moment of acceptance, uncluttered, untarnished, and unmitigated by past or future disappointment or expectation; it was a moment of absolute surrender. Surrender to what, one might legitimately ask? Why, surrender to the moment itself, of course – a full-throated commitment to Right Here, Right Now. As far as I can tell, that surrender is what is required in order to effectively navigate the heart-breaking waters of Alzheimer's protracted, debilitating, and destructive decline…

It is only fair to say that the ability to make that surrender is a hard won skill. It does not come easily or naturally, especially in the sacred context of the demise and disappearance of a cherished loved one. What we, as humans, want to do is shake our fists at the sky, curse the unfairness of life, and cling desperately to the hope of renewal, or to the images of what used to be, before the cruel imposition of such a heartless and random life levy. All of those responses are reasonable – or at least understandable – in light of the nature of the loss of something or someone so dear. Yet, as ready and palpable as those responses *are*, what they are *not* is satisfying, in any way. To rail against injustice is a purgative only for the time that one's voice is so raised; the hollow silence that follows the scream is the far more enduring signature and symbol of the dispiriting helplessness that accompanies an inescapable plight. And if there is anything that accurately describes the journey of the disease of Alzheimer's, it is the notion of an inescapable plight. It is over that sense of hopelessness that one must learn to rise, inhabit, celebrate, and surrender to the individual moments that comprise that long, exhausting path. It is in that rise that all potential joy resides…

"…*and eliminate the negative*…"

I have no clear, specific memory of the moment when I became a devotee of the popular song; I know that my youthful head was in the radio from the time I was four or five years old, because I *know* songs that I could only have heard then – songs that I have never deliberately learned, and yet I can perform them if I am asked the innocent, "Do you know...?" question. Songs seat themselves in the ever-expanding auditorium of my mind, and never relinquish their places. Some people remember numbers, or train schedules, or names, or laws of physics; I think we all have some unique trait or skill that simply comes with the package of our being, regardless of whether or not we ever discover our individual, light-bulb ability. I know what mine is, and I've known for a long time; I remember songs. I remember songs that I have no valid reason for remembering, no connect-the-dots logic that tenders some kind of unconscious significance; I remember songs simply because I heard them. Serendipitously, in my late teens, I began to learn to play guitar and discovered that I was in possession of a hitherto unknown and wide-ranging repertoire of songs of great variety. "Naturally," I thought, "I'll play; this is what I'll do; this is who I'll be, and what the mission of my life will be." Well, sort of...

Narcissism is a crippling condition; the disturbing level of self-involvement that is required to achieve almost any kind of expertise is alarming under the best of circumstances. There are those who work and study and aspire and commit because they have in mind the service of a greater good, of acquiring the skills and knowledge necessary to make a meaningful contribution to the world-at-large, or to a specific community of their choosing. Either way, the trajectory of the chosen path is one that is in service to others, and that overall beneficence overrides whatever selfishness is necessary for the achievement of the goal of exemplary competence. People such as those come few and far between; so few, in fact, that we know the names of a good many of those luminous examples: Gandhi, Buddha, Jesus, Muhammed, Martin Luther King, Nelson Mandela, Steve Jobs, Bill Gates – you get the idea… The truly exceptional, and their exceptional journeys, are well-documented, and yet, even among them are those who experienced the epiphany of the greater good only after their thirst for individual good was fully slaked. So be it – call it glass half-full… The rest of us – for the most part (myself included) – embark on journeys that are all about ourselves, often accruing significant wakes of collateral damage on the way to our not-so-clearly-defined destinations of self-aggrandizement…

For the first twenty-or-so years of my performing life (which is to say, my adult life…), such was my path and journey. Along the way, I learned – as do all performers who evidence any kind of staying power – that performance is not about you, the presenter, but is instead about the audience – the recipients of the presentation. On the surface, that would seem to be an expression of something akin to getting over one's self, but upon closer examination, it is in actuality, the toothy-grinned, near-sinister manipulation of circumstances to one's own benefit – the old, "you feel good, I do well" school of leave 'em laughing. The Faustian bargain that is entertainment success is most often kept from view; the entertained and the entertainer have an unspoken agreement that neither will ask too much of the other, because neither really wants to know the other's actual situation. It would be difficult to put on the greasepaint and make 'em laugh if the murky, sordid details of the audience's need for escape into an entertainment were known. Conversely, knowledge of the emotional and psychological dysfunctions that comprise the genuine, cumulative circumstance of a "good entertainer" does not lend itself to a greater enjoyment of the show. It is the truest, and maybe the earliest "Don't Ask, Don't Tell..." scenario. It is also one of the dark secrets of artificial, superficial joy.

> *"...And latch on to the affirmative..."*

All of that changed for me when I became a full-time dad. For the first time – in a life of exuberant self-indulgence – I found myself in the company of someone about whom I cared more than I cared for myself, someone whose needs were obviously and necessarily placed above my own; I was more than a little surprised to find how giddy that relinquishing of self made me feel. I was overjoyed at the opportunity that fatherhood presented for becoming a person of substance, and it was an opportunity I was not going to miss. What I did not know at the time was how far reaching and all encompassing that decision and commitment would be. It is often the case that we nod in assent at the initial presentation of what turns out to have been "a good idea at the time." It is far less often true that the same notion germinates into the mighty oak and becomes the central focus and anchor of one's being. A shift in perception necessitates a reciprocal shift in reality, and the more dramatic the shift, the more profound the change engendered by it. Literally overnight, I went from a life of self-indulgence to a life of utter and willing subservience, a transformation that began in the personal and particular confines of the loving new role I had so fully embraced, and grew to include all the fragile and vulnerable living creatures (which is to say, all creatures) with whom I came in contact. What was - and is – surprising to me is how seamless and easy it was to accommodate the tectonic shift from selfish to selfless, especially when that suddenly unobstructed view was made visible through the unlikely window that was an eight pound baby boy. Without hesitation, all self-deception and uncertainty about meaning and purpose were banished – along with the unhealthy and unattractive side effects that come hand-in-glove with the preoccupation with self…

Kids. Little kids, especially – are buoyant, brash, bubbling vessels of RIGHT NOW, and of future possibility, simultaneously. It appears to me – from my own experience, and what I have observed in the world – that if one opens up to genuinely loving a child, one can't help but include all children under that vast umbrella of affection and concern. Some little humans are difficult, to be sure, but those impasses are better resolved by a further opening of that umbrella than by restricting its access. In return for that adult openness, what one receives is shared joy in the excitement and pleasure of small things – small successes, small gestures, small laughter, small busy-ness of all kinds. As a performer, it is emboldening to learn that resident in those small beings is a gigantic willingness to go along with whatever is presented, as long it is presented in a way that is as uncluttered and un-self-conscious as the receivers, themselves. The result of such an unspoken bargain is the wholly circular exchange of unfettered joy with no lines of separation, no performer and audience artifice, only a broadly inclusive "we" that revels in its own antics, its own moment, its own thoroughly temporary and ephemeral Now-ness. The release of that notion of control or direction in the generous, joyful company of children was and remains a crucial, incremental step on my purposeful journey to the right here, right now insight that informs all of my moments spent in the company of older people who have lost uncountable steps along the way…

"…*and don't mess with Mr. In-Between…*"

(As a brief aside, it was my musical life performing with children that was instrumental in forging my connection with Tammy Bowers, the creator of this Inspiring Hearts Book series. When Tammy was the driving force behind **Take A Step Food Allergy Awareness***, I was fortunate to catch her ear as a children's performer, and was invited to perform at some fundraising events and benefits for that organization. I was drawn to the idea of doing something positive for kids who lived with such a frightening, heightened vulnerability that put them at such considerable risk through no fault of their own. For the organization at that time, I wrote a song about the need to spread awareness of the dangers of food allergies called, "Tell Everybody," which is exactly what we attempted to do...)*

So... once again, it is in the letting go that the greatest return is achieved. Who hasn't heard the million maudlin clichés (and their cynical parodies) exhorting us to set free what we love, let go of that which we fear, that to which we cling in the misguided hope of some (supposed) satisfaction to be achieved in a moment of righteous anger, or jealousy, or vengeful unforgiveness. We have all heard them – usually when we are least able to really *HEAR* them – and we have balked at the soothing, smarmy delivery and tone that come hand in glove with such pat counsel... We have rolled our eyes and condescendingly mimicked the expressions and the Pollyanna nature of such wide-eyed acceptance of naïve, aphoristic wisdom; at least, I know I have. But here's the thing - all of those histrionics and hip, cynical reactions don't make the clichés themselves any less true. In fact, I'm certain that is exactly how a cliché comes to be in the first place – driven by its inherent truth, which will forever outweigh and outlast all of the dark jabs that may come in response to it. We may tire of the dull repetition of a thing we are certain we already know and have already heard countless times; we may rightly say that the lustre is gone from whatever original sparkling intent and awareness once was, but none of that makes it *not so*. It is an excellent example of the surrender to right here, right now. One can summon judgment and refrain from accepting the spirit of the moment, but why would one? Would anyone in possession of reasonable empathy refuse a gift from a child? Does anyone **need** a sticky, misshapen paper clip or plastic something put into their hand? No. But, accept them we do, and smile and say, "Thank you!" because, without thinking, we surrender to the moment and meet the child exactly where the child is in his or her intent…

…You've got to spread joy up to the maximum…

Playing music for children – being in the company of children - is filled with countless moments such as those and each one presents an opportunity to further gird oneself for the hard work of letting go, of surrendering to the moment, whatever that moment may be. Because the children themselves pin the needle on the adorable meter (generally speaking), the hard work is made a trifle easier, but it is no less insistent or real. Spend enough time with children responding to their needs, their crises, and their joys, and one will be well prepared for the curves that will come when life takes the mound in earnest. Having a problem at work? At home? Anywhere? Consult a kindergarten teacher; they possess unparalleled negotiation and peace-making skills…

The long arc of life is strikingly similar at its beginning and end points, and therefore, those who say that early childhood and old age are reflections of each other are more right than wrong, I do believe. Because of those many similarities, it is a relatively simple process to take all one's accumulated knowledge of one group and modestly reshape it into very useful information about the other.

Once again, for me, the general angle of view and access point was music – specifically, the popular song. In many cases, the same popular songs are compelling at both ends of the chronologic spectrum, which is both amusing and remarkably convenient. That common repertoire, though, also provides some insight into the enduring nature of our common tastes and responses. In the middle part of our lives, we humans have a lot of rules about stuff, and music in particular – what is and isn't cool, what we do and do not like (for any number of questionable reasons), what does and doesn't enhance our place in the firmament of a desired social order and position... But at each end of this life, those rules become guidelines and they are simpler and significantly less rigid – does it feel good; does it make me smile and want to move; do I know the words? Those criteria are virtually identical at the two extremes, which makes moving from one extreme to the other seem not extreme at all... All of that has proven itself to me to be true, but the greatest benefit that is the offspring of those relaxed parameters, is that the capacity for joy is infinitely more accessible. When we humans feel less vulnerable and are less defensive, we are much more open to feeling and expressing joy. That is a bit of insight that I feel extremely fortunate to have stumbled upon and strived to understand. Minus the joy, what's the point?

"...and bring gloom down to the minimum..."

In what turned out to be the waning moments of his working life, my dad (who had been a stock broker, a financial services advisor, and had run his own golf glove company) was doing presentations at senior centers about annuity investments. In his presentations, he used a slide projector and a collapsible projection screen to add visual stimulus to an, otherwise, rather dry and lifeless subject matter. He was at a time in his life when he was not the physical dynamo he had once been, and I was working mostly at night, so he asked if I would help him schlep his hardware about to make his presentations, and I agreed, happy to have the opportunity to share the time and to assist the man to whom I owed a lot (substantively speaking) but with whom I communicated little. We would show up, cleaned up and coat-ed and tie-d; I would set up, and step aside, and my dad would hold forth, trying to impart the importance of his information, and hoping to arouse folks to act assertively in their own financial self-interests. Some of the meetings generated hoped-for sales calls; most of the meetings were sparsely attended (turns out that folks aren't that interested in acting assertively in their own financial self-interests); all of the meetings were greeted with less than enthusiastic responses, and some of the meetings' hosts would attempt to deflate the disappointment with charming, but superfluous, conversation. On one such occasion, I was asked by the meeting's hostess what I did, other than cart about and set up my father's kit. When I told her of my musical life, she asked if I had ever played for the senior population. I said, "No," but that I knew a lot of old country and swing tunes and would love to give it a shot. So, she came to see me play, and hired me to come perform for the center at which she was the director. And thus began the first leg of the journey that was to come to define, not only my performing life, but also my understanding of the immeasurable value of music in the social and emotional lives of the most vulnerable among us – who are, in truth, everyone, but who we have come to perceive as the very old and the very young…and in my – and many people's - case, my own mother…

Given the time (and substantial motivation), I think it could be novel, informative, and amusing to cobble together a collection of stories entitled, *"Epiphanies I Have Known And Loved."* I have a list, as I'm sure countless people do, of those pivotal moments of awareness that stand in stark contrast to the mundane ordinariness of most other moments, tasks, and minor achievements that are the sum and substance of our lives. One such epiphany for me occurred when I was about a year into playing, with some regularity, for the senior groups to which I had been given entrée by my acquaintance from my father's meeting. Up to that point, I had been polite, and proper, and deferential – almost to the point of reverence – as gestures of respect for the older people for whom I was playing. It was as if they were Fabergé eggs, and I had been charged with their safe and comfortable passage, for an hour, in that performance space. Therefore, my tread was both light and unremittingly cautious – it was not cheerless, but it was also not joyful. And then, the Epiphany. In mid-performance, in my head, I had this conversation with myself, "Is this how you talk and behave around your own parents? Aren't most of these people parents, as well? Haven't they experienced the same struggles, heartaches, and elations?" To which I answered, in order, "NO," "YES," and "OF COURSE!!" At that moment, precisely, the switch was flipped and I began to regard them not as Fabergé treasures, but more as hard-boiled, dyed and decorated Easter eggs, not unbreakable, but certainly not fragile and delicate. Precisely at that moment, rigid convention came tumbling down, joy made her entrance, and toil beat a hasty retreat...

> *"...Have faith or pandemonium is liable to walk upon the scene..."*

In the process of learning how to play a musical instrument (or a sport, or speak another language, or use power tools...*anything*), there is a moment of discovery on the way - after some considerable effort – when the awkwardness, the foreignness, the unfamiliarity of the task falls away for a moment, and out of the darkness of impossibility, a small light of maybe breaks, and a eureka moment of, "I GET IT!! I CAN DO THIS!!" punctuates the labor of learning. (Golfers have this moment all the time, seduced by one, two, or three good shots in a round to come back over and over again to be routinely confounded by the unimaginable difficulty of a simple game.) Needless to say, the eureka moment passes and the plodding begins anew. BUT – that occasional moment is enough to foster hope and dedication, in the face of endless, thankless travail…

This process describes exactly what occurred after my initial moment of performance epiphany; I was not suddenly fluent in this new tongue of joy. In fact there were many years yet to come when that subtle but distinct light would appear, and vanish, and reappear. In contrast, in the company of children, joy is remarkably present, without effort or question. Come with joy or openness to children, and that is how they will respond, without hesitation. There are invisible boundaries of personality and uncertainty, to be sure, but those boundaries are easily discovered, and far and away comprise a minority reaction. The same is not true of older adults with varied and undefined infirmities that must be discovered and accommodated in an instant in order to not violate the unseen border of trust and acceptance. Even the completely confused know when they are not comfortable or pleased – and, conversely, when they are. The knowledge and vision to be able to recognize those frailties and meet people (however compromised) where they are, is a wisdom acquired over time…

In my case – again – it was the popular song that informed my acquisition of that wisdom. Countless times – in the unlikeliest of circumstances – I have been witness to the emergence of sallowed faces lifting from slumped, seated, sleeping positions as if coming up from underwater, and then singing along, remembering lyrics to songs unheard in decades, long after the names of family members have retreated from memory. Those moments are profound; that joy is profound; that long ago, buried memory surfaces right here, right now at the confluence of the twin time rivers of now and then. Minus that song, there is no moment. Tears have welled in me many more times than one to watch the amazement on the faces of family members and staff when a loved one/resident/patient emerges in that way, for the briefest of moments. As profound as those moments are, they are – in some regards – mere sleight of hand tricks to orchestrate such responses. The songs are bells, and the moments are Pavlovian –to the degree that one is, indeed, that cynical. Certainly such moments are not any kind of an indicator of future behaviors or improvements that can be expected. Because of that, one could feel some disdain or disappointment for the choreographed response. One could – but one would be terribly mistaken, for this reason…

"…To illustrate my last remark - Jonah in the whale, Noah in the ark…"

Because I was playing during these moments of emergence and joy, I was being invited more and more frequently to be in the company of older adults with considerable cognitive issues, such as Alzheimer's and dementia. We had fun, and I (luckily) was comfortable in an environment where nothing is unexpected or impossible, where no boundaries or concepts such as "personal space" exist, where every learned emotional, physiological, and psychological norm has been replaced by a permanent present, in which anything is possible, at any moment. In order to navigate such unpredictable waters, one must be relaxed and comfortable, and present wholly in the moment at hand – wherever and whenever it turns out that moment may be. The men and women living in such facilities may flit back and forth between that present moment and another one 70 years ago; to attempt to understand which is which, or why, becomes a fool's errand at best, because the moment cannot be captured or explained. In the face of such rollicking, untethered movement in time, through foreign languages, ancient invisible lives, foes, and indiscretions, all one can do is occupy the moment presented at that time, for that time, and go wherever the moment goes, without attempting to understand. It is improvisational theater at its finest; it is liberating, and it allows for a door to be opened for joy to enter – surfing time on the wave of a song.

    The moment, however, that cemented forever for me the value of the popular song in such a strident context, occurred in a private hospital room, with no family, friends, or staff present. I had been asked if I would be comfortable doing bedside singing in the most dispiriting ward of a local rehabilitation hospital. Just a song or two, for those who could not come out for the group entertainment, and who in truth might never leave their rooms again. The health and physical conditions of all of these patients were dire, at best, but most were conscious and pleased to have someone sing softly to them some old familiar song. I was happy to be the messenger of such a brief, intangible moment of comfort for their weary souls, and I felt good about being able to bring that small gift. I had been in three or four rooms, and had one more that I had been asked especially to visit. I was told the patient was in bad straits, virtually unconscious, but in her former life had always enjoyed music. I entered the room quietly, and could immediately see that the lady in the bed was not conscious, was on oxygen, had tubes running in and out of every orifice, and presented strong evidence of serious stroke damage – eyes closed, mouth hanging half open, a small towel resting beneath her chin to catch the liquid that was constantly dripping from her mouth. And yet, I was supposed to sing to her - so I did. I guessed her approximate age, calculated back to the time of her adolescence, and played a song ever so softly, gently leaning in towards her head so she could hear. No response whatsoever – and, no surprise… Halfway through the song, however, I glanced down at her arm which had been lifelessly draped across her, her hand resting on the small bed table across her lap. I looked, looked away, and looked back again, to be sure. While I was playing and singing softly, her near lifeless arm was tapping out rhythm in time with my playing and she continued through to the end of the song. Unconscious, unable to speak, unable to open her eyes, unable to move without major assistance, she was tapping in time to a song that was playing and resonating in a place that no one could have predicted was still extant at all. I was stunned, moved, and forever convinced that the awesome power of the popular song as a communicative, healing tonic was – at the least - impossible to overvalue…

> *What did they do just when everything looked so dark?*
> *They said, "Man - You've got to Ac-Cen-Tchu-Ate the Positive …"*

In her former life, my mom had done the crossword puzzle in the paper every day, and was always frustrated and overjoyed with whatever she was able to complete of the Sunday NY Times puzzle. Her vocabulary and knowledge of history and current events were impressive by anyone's standards. Her jubilant spirit was beautifully expressed in her animated, dead-on accents and dialects that she could pop in and out of at will, to make a point or underscore a joke. Her laughter was rich and came easily; she was cherished by all those who got the chance to spend time in her ebullient company. The fluency of all of those things is gone, and it is not returning. But, she inhabits all of her moments with a gusto reminiscent of her former self, even in her current, radically diminished state. And it has been my lesson that if I simply jump into the moment with her, we are able to laugh, and sing together. By the way, she had a fantastic musical ear, loved the opera. played the piano, and knew hundreds of popular songs...

    And so it was, that on Thanksgiving eve, November 27, 2013, I sat on the edge of my mother's bed and the two of us sang, "Three Little Fishies In A Little Bitty Pool," "Save The Bones For Henry Jones," and "Accentuate The Positive," eight and a half years into her heartbreaking Alzheimer's diagnosis. And in that moment - that full-throated surrender to Right Here, Right Now - that free-standing moment of uncluttered, untarnished, and unmitigated acceptance, was the gift of joy delivered, unfettered and unbound... For, it is in the courageous rise to that surrender that *all* potential joy resides...

Ellis M Woodward jr., 2013

Ac-Cen-Tchu-Ate the Positive - music by Harold Arlen, lyrics by Johnny Mercer; published in 1944; several versions were recorded and released during that spiritually and emotionally exhausting, final winter of WWll...

A Journey of Love and Honor
by Adele Marie

Where am I...How did I get here and where is here... It is very hard to see, there is no light...I am opening my eyes and still I cannot see anything...I cannot remember anything...Where am I....

I have never been claustrophobic, so why am I feeling this way right now...*Relax I tell myself and just breathe*...Where am I...What is going on... Why can I not remember anything...I am trying to get up and I do not have much room around me to move, I lift my head and bang it on something above me...I try to raise my arms to feel what my head hit and I cannot reach my arms above me or move them around very well...I can only feel what is above my body...the texture is rough like wood...where am I....there seems to be a ceiling above me...I can feel it, but I cannot see it....it is very close only a few inches from my body to the ceiling above me...Where am I ...what is going on...*relax, I tell myself and just breathe*...

I cannot move my arms very well, my legs cannot bend...I feel trapped....there is no room.... Where am I ....I feel the air in which I am breathing is being cut off...*Dear God what is happening and where am I*....I start to feel all around me and all I keep touching is walls...*relax and just breathe*....everywhere I touch I feel the walls enclosing in upon me....Where am I....I cannot escape...I cannot get up and run....what is happening...where am I....*hello anyone there*...why can't you hear me...*where am I*...please someone can you hear me...*Relax and take a deep breathe*...I cannot...there is no air...I am suffocating and I cannot breathe...What is holding me down, why can't I move...what is going on...Dear God where am I.....

    Finally....Oh My God, what a relief, a rush of fresh air...I can breathe....I see a beautiful brilliant light that is shining before me...I can see...all of a sudden I am not enclosed any longer...I feel a rush of wind around me...Looking ahead of me I can see this beautiful light shining so bright that I have to cover my eyes...there, right there....there is a person, I see an outline of someone walking towards me...I can feel her, I can see her...Mom...ohhh... Mom where have you been...

    It seems like it has been eternity since I have seen you, how beautiful she is...she walks towards me with her arms outstretched and I run...I run to her and throw myself in her arms and break down and cry...I feel her warmth and strength flow through me, God she feels like heaven...I keep hearing her say *"I love you and I am right here"*...I look at her with tear stained cheeks as I tell her *"I am tired, I could not breathe Mom...I love you too"* ....She holds me close as I feel alive again. It just feels so wonderful to have her hold me, to know all of this is just a dream...a nightmare that never seemed to end...

    I feel a rush of warmth and love surge through me...I feel a cocoon of gentleness surround me and I feel safe...as I raise my head to look around I see all of my family walking up to join us...Everyone is smiling, laughing and so happy, welcoming me back...Grandma and granddaddy...Tillie and Poppi hugging me in their embrace...whispering to me " *it is over child, you are safe, no one can ever hurt you again"*...And I start to weep, finally someone heard me...someone came to my rescue and made the pain go away.... I can breathe...I feel so loved and cherished that I just want to stay there....I can finally relax and let go.... They heard me...they heard my voice calling out for help...and they came...and here I am with all of my loved ones...so many faces...so many whom I recognize that I have not seen for what seems like eternity...I start to laugh excitedly...so many whom have always been right by my side that I forgot about, I have only seen them in my dreams and meditations and here they are...front and center and they hear me....*thank you for hearing me...thank you for believing me enough to hear me...to be here with me keeping me safe and sound*...

I feel the excitement, it is swirling around me so strong and sweet...I look up just as Mother walks towards me and embraces me and says " *my child well done, you see it is all so very easy...all you had to do was let go"*...yes, yes I let go of the worry, fear, pain, terror, horror that I have been living with for so long...the bonds of imprisonment being enclosed within and no one there to hear my voice....and then............

I stepped back from everyone...*Wait... what is this all about, where am I*...I look around and everywhere I see are my loved ones...all who have passed before me...all who have lived and have died in my life...well, this is normal...I see them all the time, I talk to them all the time...but ...but this is different...I am living among them breathing just as they are...feeling, hugging and seeing them so different than I have always done...

I turn to Mother and say" *Mother where am I ...what has happened?"*...she gentle places her arms around me to see where I was... as I look around there is my physical body...it is in a box...six feet under....

Oh my God…I remember now…I could not breathe, I kept running and running and no one would listen to me…no one would hear me when I asked for help…they all just laughed…I told everyone …I kept telling them I was being stalked, I kept telling them he is out to destroy me…he hires people to follow me, to scare me and to keep the control through terror and intimidation…the abuse is never ending, they are now doing all of it legally…the abuse is now legalized abuse….No one would listen, they kept saying it will be over soon… and I kept running and then it happened…out of nowhere…. I felt a pressure and then nothing ……..

As I looked over I saw my children all standing around me crying…hurting with so much pain and anguish, all terrorized for what had happened to me…they all fell apart…they keep re-living the nightmare…..my friends where there too…each one of them crying…each one of them talking about the fight and struggle of watching it all happen to me when no one would listen…But no one would move so I could see what had happened to me…I remembered seeing this and thinking *why are you crying for me…I finally feel good, I am free from the abuse and fear of being assassinated…no fear…no terror…no watching over my shoulder to see where it was coming from…no more can they hurt me…no more can they control or abuse me…*I was in that box…six feet under…….

But then the rush of emotions to know Dear God what now…my children are not safe…I was not safe and now they are all alone to have to fight that same threat of fear and terror…my antagonist got what they wanted …they stalked me and they got rid of me and now what will happen to my children…I curled up in a ball and wept…I cried out against the injustice of what had happened…I hurt all over because like me, there was nothing they could do…no one to turn to …nowhere to hide….no justice for the abused, for those who fear for their lives...the systems do nothing to help, they close their eyes and ears to the cries around them...for it is not their life, it is not their family and it is not their problem....

He did this...his family did this and his counsel did this...the world allowed this to happen because no one would listen...they would not listen to my words...my voice...my side of the story...I never hurt anyone...I always lent a helping hand...I could never stay mad at anyone and never judge another....I took the abuse for years...I swallowed my pride on numerous occasions. I gave in to keep the hurt and pain away from others...I allowed myself to be blackmailed, threatened, terrorized, manipulated, living in fear each day and still I gave with so much love as to not harm another....why...why does society allow this to continue...

All I did was say *"I am tired and through...I want out"*...I want out of the hell I was living in...constantly being told how much a piece of crap I was, constantly being told that no one cared about me...constantly stepping between him and the kids so he would not keep hurting them with his cruel remarks and twisted behavior...Constantly having to give him my money so he could buy whatever he thought he needed with no thought to others...constantly being humiliated for my femininity and having to submit on demand, Constantly being the whipping post when he learned a new karate move...constantly being told how dumb and stupid...that I was *"no fun"* because I did not drink...and all the times when a gun was kept pointed to my head as I went to bed...Constantly the beer flowed around him, every day every night watching as he drank more and more...watching as he doctored himself with his own medications. It was never ending and then I made the mistake to say *I want to be left alone I want out of this marriage*...

And then it began and this time more in earnest…this time it was worse than ever before, the taunting, the threats, objects being thrown and stolen…the belittling by him and his family…all the lies, the untruths…their imagination was going wild….busting through the door to the house to intimidate, threaten and even more lies…watching as they went to court and gave under oath untruths upon untruths…sworn testimonies to take my children away from me with lies…my mouth dropping open as they knew they were lying…I remember thinking " *God is going to get you for all of your untruths…how can you live with yourself by being so untruthful*"…the stalking day and night continues…the phone calls continue…my friends and their families receiving calls scaring them, threatening them…my phone being wiretapped…a tracking device on my truck so that at any hour of night and day they would know my whereabouts…never being alone to be at Peace…to feel safe……

All those years of me being alone trying to help him fight his battle with alcohol and addiction to his prescriptions meds and his family would close their eyes and ears to the truth, to the abuse that the children and I lived through, allowing their grandchildren to live through that pain because they were not going to admit their son had problems….oh no…for that would mean that they had a hand in their sons faults and no one in that family had any faults…they were all perfect….they left me to deal with their son and his addictions and they walked away, but not before they would say how much they hated me…why…was I getting too close to the truth…because I told the truth even though they would not listen… they did not live in reality… but that which was their own…

I would always hear… "it's your lie you tell it…well, they tell it so very well"…

And here I am six foot under…in a box in the ground and no one can hear my voice any longer…no one can hear about the injustice that we as abuse victims live through…no one has to look upon my face any longer to see truth in my expressions and to hear my words of truth about the horrors I lived through…you see if they did…they would know what truth really is…and not just that of a delusional woman who felt every pain that was inflicted upon her…A woman who could no longer take the mental, emotional, sexual, financial and physical abuse and pain any longer…that she decided to voice her words…she decided to be a voice that others could hear so they too would find comfort in knowing they are not alone…

Statistics show that abused women and men return to their abuser as no one will hear their voice, their side of the story…that the justice system is designed to have the abused go back to the abuser so that they (the justice system) does not have to be involved in domestic violence…you may see many shows on television about abuse…time and again, someone losing their life as the justice systems says there is no threat or you must have total proof of evidence, we call that death. The here and after of seeking help and being turned away. But to have the real story unfold would relate a true society that turns it back upon the nurturers of life, the ones that hold it together, the ones that are brow beaten into keeping the mouths shut. No one wants the truth displayed so blatantly as the systems which uphold prejudices would have to start answering to the population the questions of why. Why do we have a civilization with a justice system to uphold equality to all living beings, turn a blind eye to those in bondage to the rage of an abuser? That which we have to continually suffer through to prove to a single human being sitting high above their perch, looking down upon us, most times tired of hearing about suffering in which they themselves either never experience or have been the abuser at one time in their life. To then pass the judgment of no wrong doing to the perpetrator of malicious harm, to only be told that there is not enough evidence to convict, not enough to give a sliver of hope that the abused may just have a supporter, someone who understand, someone who shall protect them. Sadly the systems in which we have to live by every day, fails time and time again. No one is willing to show you the real horrors and truths the abused go through or has to live through just to take another breath and to keep alive one more day. The only thing the system knows is not that which shall free the abused from the bondage, but that which throws the abuser the key to continue as never before. The system is set up to look the other way…to give just enough assistance to keep the abused stringing along with enough hope that unfortunately never comes along.

For no one understands the abuser will always find ways to keep that voice from being heard………and knows they can get away with it…….

And to those who find the courage to say *"enough is enough, I am getting out"*…just look six feet under and know they are still there just waiting for someone to hear their voice.

Every day is continues and every day we live among thousands of individuals experiencing one form or another of abuse and their voices are never heard until we see their pictures in the news media headlines. We cling to the illusion that everything is good in our world, even when we are confronted by it within our own households, schools, businesses, worship groups, book clubs, playgrounds, tennis courts, shopping malls, restaurants, every aspect of our life. There is not place on Mother Earth that there is not someone, somewhere being abused. Abuse does not discriminate between male or female, young or old, black or white, suburbs or cities, east coast or west coast and everywhere in between worldwide. There are no boundaries as this has been a world epidemic for as far back as we can go in history.

Many times writing this I had to walk away as it is a very emotional and shameful experience to go thru, to admit you were victimized with abuse, as I could see why so many turn their back and succumb to the degradation all over again. It is very humiliating to know you allowed yourself to succumb to another individual's power over you. Here you are educated, smart, gentle, passionate about what you do and who you are, to then realize that there is so many other layers upon which you have hidden deep within. It's a journey of understanding what abuse is and how the mainstream world only focuses upon the physical attributes and not the emotional and mental, sexual or financial aspects of abuse.

It has taken me three long years of mourning, mourning of everything in my life and that of the individual I loved, to get here now behind this desk writing these words. And when I keep getting up and walking away from it, it is still there as the words pour through my heart and mind, but I am refusing to claim them on paper. For to do so is a giving of myself and energy to that which I am no longer a part of. Allowing it once again to come alive, once again the opportunity to swallow me whole, until I realize we are no longer within the controlling confides of another, but to which we are our own master forever more. So here I sit, determined to follow thru on a commitment I made to myself and that was to love myself with all my heart as I deserve no less. And yes, it is a mourning period that has lasted as long as I allowed, as like many I would keep pushing it away, refusing to acknowledge it for what it was. A time of mourning all the hopes, dreams, love and time that I had given to making things work, to giving my love to someone that never realized how to cherish such a precious gift. A finality of knowing that whatever my aspirations for a long and happy marriage were, they never materialized into the American dream as so many of us long for.

As young ladies we seek that knight in shining armor that shall love us unconditionally and ride off with us into the sunset of happily ever after. Only to be shattered by the reality in this world in what it takes to make the commitment to go the distance. A distance I gave for over eighteen years of building a family home and structure of love that just could not withstand the excessive pain of cruelty any longer.

    And that is where I would constantly overlook all the realties that I was actually facing, concentrating on making it work, loving not only my husband, but giving everything I had to the well-being of my children and those around me. Making sure everyone was okay and not touched/tainted by the truth of the ugliness in which we lived. Moreover humiliating to think that I might have failed miserably in that area as a mother, the anguish and pain I go thru with all the thoughts and emotions of saying I should have left sooner. For knowing what I know now, even though I gave it my all, I still had been in that protection mode from the one person I should not have had to protect them from. So instead thru the years I stood between the tempests of the storm that reared its ugly head to strike us down, as I was constantly reaching out to build them up. Like many thinking it is only a bad day, tomorrow will be better. He is a bi-polar maniac depressive alcoholic and I, like many before me, have told ourselves, I can help him. I laugh a little at that now, because no matter the years of making the appointments for him to go to the counselor/shrink, to driving him there to even sitting in his sessions to explain what he was going thru, I was still delusional. Here he sat time after time making me talk for him, as I knew if I did not do so, what the consequences would be on the drive home. Stopping at the liquor store as he bought more beer so he could laugh triumphantly as he believed he got over on his counselor/shrink. Hiding away and allowing the alcohol to numb him to his own pain. Pain that was brought on by his own upbringing in which his parents gave to him; the love and acknowledgements that he so craved from his parents that they just did not deliver to him. For years I watched the hatred pour out of him when he talked to them and about them. Never calling them mom or dad, but always by their given names. Who did this? Only someone who had emotional distanced themselves from the individuals who had hurt them the most, his parents. And since they could not deliver what he so desperately needed from them he took it out on those who were unknowingly willing to give him what he searched for. Love and understanding, support and a shoulder to lean on and to tell him he is a great person.

Still, it did not really hit me how far gone I was into his matrix of reality and that of my own reality that I was an abused spouse until he said a simple statement of honesty that as an alcoholic or addict he will say to me all the ugly things he thinks in his mind about himself. He will tell me things and make me believe it is all me, as that is really how he feels about himself. He feels cheap, ugly, disgusting pig, fat, dumb, liar, stupid, (and all varieties the other horrible words he used to describe about me that cannot be printed here). All of these words and demeaning values were what he really felt about himself and since he could not fight himself with all of it, he then knew he could project that upon us to make it more real to be able to fight us, which in his own mind was himself. You see now it is a more tangible living breathing thing that he has created and as we accepted it over and over again, he could keep giving it to us as we were now the material equivalent to him. So he never felt any compunction not to keep doing it, to not see what he was creating, he was so blinded by the anger and hatred that festered deep inside of his own self over his relationship to his family. And when he came at you, it was better to let him do what he was going to do and get it over quickly then try to fight back. The peace was worth waiting for. That would be why at times when his family came to visit and he started going off yelling and smashing things that they would walk out the door leaving us with their laughter and words of "better you than me". Leaving us to deal with the aftermath alone, the ones they professed to love so much, once again hurt and confused by their betrayal.

So as we journey thru the matrix of understanding reality it hit me one day, that there is a tie to everything I had been shown thru the years. Running rampant in my mind were little pictures, glimpses of history, seeing him in other times, listening to his words as his actions followed suit, videos running rampant in my mind of both us. Snatches of other time and places where he was lord and master and everyone followed his bellowing his orders, his preferences always asking myself… "what/who is he and where do I come in?". And then I would see her standing on top of a mountain pass, her hair blowing in the wind wearing a suit of armor. And she would point over the mountain and I could see a place where many were gathered. Hundreds upon hundreds of souls all in suits of armor with a flag that was so large that read "House of Joan" with a large red cross and I would knell down and thank her for pointing the way. And then of course I would start to laugh as my mother's name was the same, and it was her house within I had grown and the similarities were very overwhelming as she too was a fighter in this life, but for as much deeper enemy called cancer. So what does it all have to do with me? I had started the emotional healing journey harder than I had ever before; I was in the middle of writing a manuscript when it hit me so hard I could not breathe.

I too was a wounded warrior in the House of Joan and I had survived all of the onslaught of his abuse before in another time in another place. And just as before, I was his victim in this lifetime to control, use and rule. And then too, I was a warrior and I was humbled to know I had survived then and I shall survive now. I just needed to finally wake up, open my eyes and live for once in my life without his abuse and control. I had to make the hard choice of finally accepting it was over, all the years of his and his families abuse that they had inflicted upon my and mine, all the years of not being able to breathe and live like a free person, one who had a freedom of rights in this lifetime. And as I started the journey up that hill they brought the most un-dignified and ugliest battle they could. I, just as before, made a pact to not lower myself to the insidious depravation that a human would sink to, to get what they wanted, mind you not what they needed, but what they truly believed and wanted for their own selfish greed. The more they threw at us and tried to take from us by trying to kill my daughter, they more God rumbled. The more they took, they more they gave out to others, all of my personal information, that information that can change your life by someone falsifying and using your identity to do harm and ugliness, they more God's hand wrapped around us. The more untruths, deceptiveness and slander the more God's promise would scream in my ears "They may get their monetary due, that which is all they craved, but one day they shall rue when they come face to face with me". So we kept going, I knew as a wounded warrior before that there shall be trials and tribulations but we shall walk away with God's blessings and love upon us. We let them do all that they did without one time returning the same vehemence as was projected upon us. We stayed in or truth and allowed God to lead us on our journey.

So too, did Joan allow God thru his messengers of Archangel Michael, Saint Margaret and Saint Catherine to lead the way. So too, did Joan show the way for many wounded warriors as they gathered to refresh and regroup their souls to that of the journey in which Gods showed the way and gave Grace to all who heeded the word of God and so too, do we still gather this day. I have met many wounded warriors of the House of Joan and I find that I know them instantly when we meet. These beautiful souls who give so much of themselves to help those with whom they know are living with deep anguish inside or in living in pain. To help ease them, to assist them to be able to live among the living once again. The warriors from the House of Joan are here to assist humanity and those whom have been thrown away as if they never existed to begin with.

You see, on the other hand, you have those in pain seek these beautiful souls to assist them in their own cleansing and healing journey, they try to capture that purity, that healing, that compassion, love, grace and mercy for themselves, stealing it like a thief in the night and crush it to its very soul and then explode in anger when they have destroyed the one good in their life. Never to breathe again, no longer having that goodness next to them. No longer being able to pull the essence of that love and purity deep within their soul and their soul then sours and suffers mightily. They will then need another; the search begins anew for their next victim, their next beautiful soul to suck dry before the soul realizes what happened. For you see every soul awakens when it is deep within the trench believing it is too late to escape. But it is never to let to live, it is never too late to escape and breathe once again your true original soul self. The soul then like a phoenix explodes to be born all over again.

I thank you for taking the time to read these words written upon this paper, the journey is more than complicated, it is never truly done. We have the choice to either allow others to take away our freedom, our voice, and our soul or to take the journey with God and allow God to lead the way with Love. They acquired what they coveted most, the house and all their greedy money, I received the greatest gift out of the whole process, my children living free and happy to be able to make their own choices and to be who they truly are here to be…Loved.

We live each day knowing we are free from harm, control, lies, viciousness, hatred, and so much more, that all of this is a journey of souls uniting together bringing back the House of Joan to stand stronger than ever before. And we a truly grateful each day that God guided us through it all, for our faith never died, just that of old souls coming back together again.

There are those with whom you pass along the street each day that are from the House of Joan, they are the beautiful souls who have lived thru many disruption and ridicule in their life, they have weathered the storm and continue on. Never asking for anything but always giving, never seeking but always there, never given the chance to tell their stories to those who really care. But they are the ones in our society that bear the bruises and broken bones, the mental and emotional break downs, seen and unseen of those who seek to destroy any love or beauty in the world, and I bless them and send them my love for being the wounded warrior in our world. For you see if they had not chosen to dedicate this lifetime to helping and assisting others without thought to their own self, then you would have that on your doorstep even more.

Next time your friend, daughter, son, student, mother, father, sister or brother, coworker or someone that acts or says something that makes you stop to think, makes you question anything different about them than what you have always known…open your eyes a little more and share this with them and then ask…Can You Relate?… and if they try to change the subject or make an excuse, let them know that they are not alone and you really do understand. Take time to take their hand and quietly walk them away and show them that life is for living...Let them know about the House of Joan and how they are special, too special, to be left alone anymore on their own...that they no longer have to do it all on their own...For it is thru awareness in knowing their lives are so valuable and treasured that we can save them from being front page news and then our job here is done. God Bless

"Welcome to the House of Joan, wherein lies your journey to living life once again"...

Love, Laughter & Light™, Adele Marie
2014©Adele Marie/Angelic Wise Ones
All Rights Reserved

* * *

Destiny

by Drema Bonavitacola

We are all empowered by the spirit within.
We must light the fire, take the first step,
and begin....

This is as good as it gets. Each day brings the sun and each night sky is soaked with stars. I am left to fill each new day, learning to live without him. This journey forward is not easy and some days it is hard just getting out of bed, but through hardships there are lessons to be learned, messages to be given, and many blessings to be realized.

It was a warm September afternoon when my life as a mother forever changed. The devastating news was delivered by two policeman that beautiful sunny day. How do I recover from the death of my baby, my 18 year old son? This gut-wrenching ordeal was real. Feeling enveloped, tossed, pushed and overwhelmed by this sudden shock, an unthinkable grief journey was now forced upon me. How do I go on? How can I live without my son? How can I face another day, and do I even want to?

It has been a little over a year since that unforgettable day, and yes, I am still here. I am alive and know now that I will survive. I realized that giving up was and never is an option. I am a wife, a mother, a daughter, a sister, an aunt, a friend, a co-worker, and a person... I am me, however, forever changed. I have been awakened with a new insight, a new outlook on life, a new way to view the world around me. I've been humbled and truly feel an unconditional love that has surrounded me; lifting my spirits as I have tried to live each day with this love light shining for all to see. I have been blessed, so very blessed.

There is true, absolute love expressed and witnessed each and every day. God has never left my side as he is ever present in the faces and actions of my incredible husband, family and friends. Their support, kindness and continued love has been what has sustained me and helped me to put one foot in front of the other, moving forward and truly seeing what life is all about. The sky is bluer, the birds sing sweeter, and the wind blows softer across my face. I have always looked at each new day with a sense of awe, but now I actually have a renewed appreciation for each sunrise and each sunset as I stand to gaze upon the glorious masterpiece while soaking up the uniqueness of each and every day. Daily blessings are what keep me going as I take each healing step. I've learned to forgive, to love, to live in the light with purpose, conviction and truth.

Of course, I didn't just wake up one day and decide to be happy, and my being happy was not going to make me feel guilty or imply that I am over the death of my son. I will never be over that life altering event, but I am going to live my life being the best that I can be. I realized that I was being carried by faith and held up by love. This was going to be a new, heartfelt journey with my eyes wide open as I carry his loving memories in my heart forever. I have been knocked down, but I have gotten back up, dried my tears and dusted off my wilted spirit. I must now be in the present, be in the now. I must inspire others to not give up, to carry on in the face of tragedy. To understand that we are stronger than we think we are and are capable of many wonderful things. We just have to look deep within to find those precious gifts, but they are there. Be still and listen, you will know what I mean.

From grief to giving, from misery to fame… I believe that our destiny is of our own doing. We create our own happiness; we are in charge of where we are going and who we are to become. Before we can help others, however, we must first take a good look at our self. We must then be diligent to preserve our mind, our body, and our soul. The essence of time brings to mind what is actually important in discovering the mystery of life. We must take time to dance, to sing, to walk in the woods, to smell the flowers, to listen to a baby's laugh and to spend time with each other, as time is so very precious.

A positive attitude along with a true intention of what is wanted out of life will take you far. Visualizing and a true belief in the future will surprisingly catapult you into a new dimension, a new life, and a new way to view the world around you. We are here to help one another. We are all connected just as the stars are up in the sky, so too are we, held together by a common thread, a bond.

I had to face and walk through this raw, sickening pain in order to reach where I am today. Grief is exhausting and relentless. I had to cry a million tears and some days this wounded warrior still does, but I will not be defined by my son's death, nor will I let sadness take away my fond loving memories of him. I have emerged a new me, I refuse to run and hide. I have taken a stand to live, to be, to love and to see… all there is to see. There is nothing more painful than the loss of a child. I have had my fair share of loss to know. We all grieve differently, but when you have given all you are and all that you have into a child, and he dies… you don't just grieve his loss, but you grieve the past, the why's, the present, the how's and the future, the what could have been. There is not going to be a college graduation, a new job, a fiancé, a wedding, a new home, or grandchildren, and the list goes on and on and on.

It is by the loving grace of God, my faith, the many blessings and prayers from family and friends that have lifted me up through the darkest of times. I could have been devastated by this, but I chose to live for my son. I chose to love for my son. And I chose to be at peace for my son. True greatness comes from within. We all have it. The potential, the ability, the desire to be whatever "it," is…Some of us never find our true authentic self. We spend our entire lives looking for happiness, or love, something that we think will make us better or that we think we need. "It," is right in front of you. It is the beating of your heart, it is the blink of your eyes, the very breath that you take. We must first just slow down, feel, listen, and see all that there is around us. Make a connection to the notes in the song, the words in a book, or to a verse in the rhyme and rhythm of life. There is a peace, a wisdom, and a truth that lies in each of us. Believing in yourself, your future endeavors, your dreams and your visions will bring a universal promise.

Forgiveness of self and others is the first step to finding the harmony that renders us peace. Gratitude and love are also needed as we find our true pathway to a joyful life. Be an inspiration, find a purpose, and embrace that which was given, learn from it and move forward with a song in your heart and a light that shines for all to see. Be patient and dream big. Take comfort in knowing that a bleeding heart will one day smile again, the sun will rise and set, and the stars will be your guide…you will know where you are going with new hope as you embark on a peaceful beginning filled with endless possibilities. Acknowledge and accept this new journey, as it will bring you total freedom to be the person you were always meant to be…. With great confidence… I welcome you to your destiny.

Author: Drema Dee Bonavitacola
February 24, 2014

Words

These letters I have written
Become words for all to read
Broken hearted messages
Perhaps so you don't bleed
Each tired journal entry
Each loving verse composed
Becomes a familiar story
That everybody knows…..
2/14/14
Author: Peace Owl

* * *

Destiny

Please don't be sad
Don't shed a tear
I've been watching you
I am always near.
Free is my spirit
I'm happy as can be
There is so much love here
And someday you will see
So be good to yourself
And kind to each other
Take care of your friends,
Your siblings, your father and mother
As angels, there's only so much
We can do
You have free will of choice
The rest is up to you
The choices you make
Can rob your destiny
Cut short your life
As well you can see
Take heed to live clean
And in the positive light
Life is so worth living
And so worth the fight….

2/9/14   Peace Owl

About the Author: Drema Dee Bonavitacola/ Peace Owl

I have always been a positive person, fun loving, generous and kind. I grew up in a small Pennsylvania town and lived with my mother and 3 sisters, in a 2 bedroom apartment. My mother worked 3 jobs to raise her girls and between us, we shared a whole lot of love, even though we didn't live in the big house on the hill. We had each other. She was my rock; my everything. Suddenly, 2 days before Christmas, a heart attack took her from me; I was 27 years old. I lost part of myself that day. I miss her and think of her every day, but I know that she is, and will always be with me. When I was 18 years old, I met my soul mate, we married 2 years later and have been married for 34 years. He is an amazing man and my best friend. We took our time getting to know each other, and after 11 years of marriage, we had our first son, and then two years later, we had our second son. Those days of raising little ones went by so fast. In a blink of an eye, I turned around and they both were handsome, young men. One in college and the other just graduated from high school. Through the years there were times when things didn't always run so smooth, but together, with our strong faith and love for each other, we found our way through the trials and issues that face many young families. We did the best we could. My husband and I were involved in our church, the boy's sports and school activities, and in their lives…I had the perfect life, the perfect family. Then all of a sudden, I was blind-sided by the death of my son, it was hard to watch the sadness engulf our entire family, our lives. It was tough to pick each other up when we were trying to help ourselves cope with the unimaginable loss. Comfort was found in prayer, looking at old photographs, reminiscing, about days gone by, the many books on grief and the out pouring of love from family and friends. I have experienced, first hand, the grace of God in the faces of those who reached out to support and continue to comfort us in our time of grief. The pain of losing my son, runs deep in my veins and some days, it still rears its ugly head. Although my son is gone, he will never be forgotten, no matter how difficult or painful it is to remember. Carry him near and dear to my heart… I will…always.

Full Hands / Full Heart
by Stacey Stirmer

On May 5th, 1994 Jake Tyler was born. It was my easiest and by far the quickest birth of all three of my children. Rather uneventful except for his umbilical cord being around his neck. The doctor quickly removed it and he let out his first cry loud and clear. Jake was a "perfect" baby. He was quiet and content. Very low maintenance. He only cried when he was hungry or needed a diaper change. His siblings, Jenna and Corey adored him.

Looking back at his early months, nothing seemed out of the ordinary except for his eyesight. I never felt like he was able to focus on my face when I talked to him. He also was slow to respond to his name, but would eventually. I justified this as third child syndrome.

The next few months Jake seemed to develop normally. He was able to pick up small pieces of food and feed himself earlier than others of the same age. He started to say "Mama" and "Dada" right on target. Again, he was a very easy baby.

At around fifteen months of age, we got our first red flags that something might not be quite right with Jake. We took him to the pediatrician for his regular well baby check up and the doctor was concerned that he wasn't trying to pull himself up to walk around the furniture. After much discussion, I realized that I hadn't heard him try to talk in a while. He seemed to have lost what little language he had learned. Jake's doctor decided that further evaluation was needed to see what was going on with him. And so our journey began.

The first step was to see a neurologist. He had a hearing test and an MRI, both under sedation. Both tests showed normal results.

The neurologist was slightly puzzled but said that in her opinion Jake did not have autism because of the way that he related to me. It was a major relief, but still a puzzle. However, I was in the public library one day in April, and they had a poster for Autism Awareness month. After reading the signs of autism on the poster, a light bulb went off in my head. That was it! My son has autism. He seemed to fit the description to a T! But the question remained, was the neurologist right or was I?

The next step was what is called a Unified Developmental Evaluation. It consisted of a six-hour appointment in which Jake was seen and evaluated by a team of professionals including a psychologist, a developmental pediatrician, a speech pathologist, a physical therapist, an occupational therapist and a neurologist. It was a grueling day as you can imagine. One of the things that they did was to purposely frustrate him to see how he reacted. It was heartbreaking to witness them "tormenting" my child!

The team was supposed to discuss amongst themselves then call us back into the room for their collective opinion on a diagnosis. Instead, we were told that they didn't have time to do this and that they would call us when they could. That meant more waiting.

A few days later, after my repeated phone calls to them, the doctor finally called me back and very bluntly told me that my son has moderate to severe autism and moderate mental retardation as well. And there it was: The diagnosis that we had searched for yet the results that we feared so much. Our son would never lead a normal life, no matter what we did to try to help him. So the next phase of our journey began.

Our son has autism! A million questions went running through our minds! What does this mean? How will it affect him? How will it affect our family? How do we keep him safe? How do we help him to reach his full potential? How will we even know what his full potential is? It was totally overwhelming!

Autism is a complex developmental disability. It is known as a spectrum disorder. No two people with autism will have the exact same symptoms. Those afflicted have various combinations of symptoms. Children with autism may have problems with communication, social skills, and reacting to the world around them. Some present more severely than others. Some people with autism are able to live fairly normal lives and others are profoundly affected.

According to Autism Speaks (An autism science and advocacy organization):

- Autism now affects 1 in 68 children and 1 in 42 boys.
- Autism prevalence figures are growing.
- Autism is the fastest-growing serious developmental disability in the U.S.
- Autism costs a family $60,000 a year on average.
- Autism receives less than 5% of the research funding of many less prevalent childhood diseases.
- Boys are nearly five times more likely than girls to have autism.
- More children are diagnosed with autism each year than with cancer, aids and diabetes combined!
- There is no medical detection or cure for autism.

The number of children diagnosed with autism is growing at an alarming rate! Researchers are trying to figure out if this is partly due to increased awareness and accuracy in the diagnostic process or if it's really that big of an increase of children on the spectrum. Nobody is certain what causes autism. Current thinking is that it's caused by a combination of factors, including but not limited to, genetic vulnerability, environmental toxins, certain types of infections, ages of parents, and problems before, during or after birth.

Now back to our story. We had to tell our family and friends that Jake would never be like a typical kid. I didn't want to think of him as disabled, but instead as differently-abled. I didn't want anybody to look at him as broken, or as anything other then the perfect child that I still saw him as being. He was still my son. He was still my Jakey boy.

It took a while for everything to sink in. We actually took the time to mourn what could have been and began to accept what would be instead. We accepted that Jake would never be the bright student that his sister was or the great athlete that his brother was, but he would find his niche and it was our job to make sure that he did.

After several more professional evaluations to try to establish a starting point, we were ready to help Jake start his new chapter. We felt that it was important to keep him challenged but not push him to the point of frustration. He attended several different programs that the public school system provided which was a great starting point. But was it enough?

We had begun hearing about a new teaching method that seemed to be working with children with autism. It was called "Discrete Trial". Around the same time, we heard that the public school system in our county was considering funding a trial program of this method. After several phone calls, more evaluations and lots of paperwork, we got Jake accepted into this trial program. He would be part of the first group of kids in Howard County to be given the opportunity to receive this type of training. The school system would provide the training and the funding as well. Our hopes were high that this intensive training would be as effective for Jake as it has been for others like him.

In a nutshell, Discrete Trial is a method of teaching that is conducted one on one between a child and a specially trained instructor in a distraction free environment. The environment selected for us was our home. With this method each task is broken into smaller components and repeated over and over again until the bigger picture is accomplished. For example: If teaching the student how to complete a jigsaw puzzle, the first step would be to present the puzzle intact with only one piece missing. Once the student is able to put that particular piece back into the puzzle where it belongs then a second piece is removed along with the first piece. The number of pieces removed increase until the student can accomplish the entire puzzle unassisted. Prompts are used in the beginning and then are gradually faded until no longer needed for each task. Prompts can be verbal, gestural, or hand over hand. It's very intense and exhausting for both instructor and child.

The county school system hired an advisor to help us set up our home program. We were told how to prepare for her arrival. We hired a team of instructors, bought our supplies and transformed our basement into a Discrete Trial classroom. Our initial training took three six-hour days which were intense and exhausting! Our advisor left and our program began.

The program ran seven days a week for six hours each day. We had a rotating team of instructors coming in and out of our home constantly. I took several shifts a week as well. One parent was required to be in the house at all times during instruction. Our advisor returned every six weeks to check Jake's progress and tweak the program accordingly.

The program was very helpful to Jake, and he made a lot of progress. The advisor also implemented a toilet training drill, which was successful! Before aging out of the program at five years old, he progressed to be able to spend half of the day with the instructor accompanying him to public school, and the other half of the day back in the basement classroom. After "graduating" from the home program, he became a full time student in the MINC program (Multiple Intensive Needs Class) in the public school system.

Today Jake is 20 years old. He is in a public high school in an ALS (Academic Life Skills) program. He has his core subjects in the special education classroom, and is integrated with his typically developing peers for lunch and various activities. He also participates in the work enclave program. He learns work skills in the school work lab and also goes out into the community to work at various jobsites while being accompanied and supervised by school staff.

Jake has lots of outside interests. He loves to bowl and attends a weekly special needs bowling league held by the parks and recreation department. He also bowls and plays indoor softball for his high school allied sports program. Allied sports is a wonderful program that allows both special needs kids and typical kids who aren't able to make a varsity team compete in a relaxed non-competitive environment. They are supplied with uniforms, bus transportation, and an end of the year sports banquet and awards ceremony. Jake even received a varsity letter! It is awesome to be able to sit on the sidelines with the other parents and cheer on our kids!

Jake also loves to swim, especially in the ocean. This past summer he had a wonderful opportunity to go surfing with an organization called Surfer's Healing. Israel Paskowitz, a professional surfer who has a son with autism, founded the organization. He took his son into the ocean on a surfboard and realized the calming effect that it had on his child. He wanted others with autism to be able to experience that feeling as well. His organization travels to various beaches across the country and takes children with autism into the ocean on surfboards. Everyone on the beach cheer for these children as they ride the waves into shore. Jake, although hesitant at first, LOVED it! They took him out a few times. He will be participating again this summer.

Another favorite activity of Jake's is to play outside. He sits on the ground for hours throwing leaves into the air and watching them fall…over and over again. He is outside in all temperatures, and often stays out until dark. We are fortunate to have a wooded backyard surrounded by a six-foot fence so that he can play safely without close adult supervision.

One of the biggest challenges that we face is associated with health care. When Jake was much younger, he started screaming out in pain and was not able to give us any clue as to what hurt him so badly. The doctor's couldn't figure out what was wrong. It could have been anything from his head down to his feet. A migraine or an ingrown toenail! We ended up in the emergency room where he was eventually diagnosed with a kidney stone. Of course he had to go under general anesthesia to have a CT scan because he would not lay still. Actually, he wouldn't even lie on the table. Fortunately, the stone passed on it's own and he was fine after that.

Whenever Jake needs any type of medical procedure or dental work he needs to go under anesthesia. He is a gentle child unless he feels threatened. If so, he will fight to protect himself, and, at five foot eleven and 229 pounds he is super strong! He's been put under twice in the last five years and both times were very traumatic. It took seven people in the operating room to try to restrain him long enough to put the mask on his face for ten full seconds. This mask was used just to knock him out enough to start the IV sedation. He was absolutely terrified and he put up one heck of a fight. It was heartbreaking as a parent to not only witness this but to help to restrain him as well. The first time, the staff actually called in hospital security to stand by in the recovery room in case he woke up combative, which fortunately he did not.

Last year, I got a phone call from school that absolutely shook my world! It was his teacher. She was clearly upset and she told me that Jake just had a grand mal seizure. She said that she had already called 911 and told me to get there as soon as I could! I rushed over to find two ambulances and a fire truck with their lights on in front of the building. The school secretary met me at the door and rushed me to his classroom. What I saw when I got there was terrifying! Jake was lying unconscious on the floor with a huge knot on his forehead. Three paramedics were working on him! What the heck was going on? He was seventeen years old and had never had a seizure before!

Jake was released from the hospital several hours later and was referred to a neurologist. We were told that some people have an unexplained seizure sometime during their lifetime. Maybe there was a reason for his, but maybe there was not. The plan was to wait and see if it ever happened again and if so we would take it from there. He was also given prescriptions for two rescue drugs to be administered if he happened to have another seizure that lasted for five minutes or longer. We were told not to leave him unattended in unsafe situations, such as in a bathtub as he could drown, or on a ladder as he could fall, etc. We were also told to make sure that he got plenty of rest, ate well and stayed as healthy as possible. We were pretty shaken, but my defense mechanisms convinced me that this was going to be a "once and done" for Jake.

At this point, Jake was getting ready to turn eighteen, an adult in the eyes of the law. What this meant was that even though he has an extreme cognitive disability, he would be responsible for his own health care decisions. If he didn't request medical care or consent for treatment he would not receive any. Here is a child who cannot write or even say his own name, but he would have to sign to consent for treatment. That's crazy! After talking with the transition specialist at school and consulting with an attorney, we decided to go to court to request medical guardianship of Jake. We hired an attorney, Jake was assigned a court appointed attorney, and we had two doctors fill out forms and then had a hearing in court. Fortunately our request was granted. Now we can make sure that all of Jake's medical needs will be met!

On December 31st, 2012 my husband and I were sitting in our family room discussing our plans for New Year's Eve later that night. Our older son Corey was home from college for the holidays and all was good in our home. All of a sudden we heard a very loud thump from upstairs. We looked at each other slightly puzzled, and then continued our conversation. Shortly after came a second loud thump! When I realized the possible reason, it felt like my heart jumped out of my chest and I ran upstairs. I was actually scared to open Jake's bedroom door for fear of what I might see! I opened it slowly, but something was the way. I pushed it open and found Jake on the floor against the door in a semi-conscious state. He collapsed as I tried to brace his fall. I screamed for my husband and together we were able to lay him flat so that he could breathe better. We then realized that all of the noise was poor Jake having another seizure! By the time we got upstairs the seizure was over, but he received another concussion because of hitting his head on his dresser. Aside from vomiting twice, Jake was out cold for about six hours afterward. I was told that this is normal because the brain is exhausted from the trauma.

We set up another appointment with his neurologist for later that week. It was at that appointment that Jake was officially diagnosed with epilepsy. He never had a seizure until he was seventeen years old, and now he had developed epilepsy! The plan was to put him on a new anti-seizure medicine. We were told to watch him very closely as this medicine could potentially have serious side effects. One of those side effects was a sudden onset rapidly spreading rash that could be as severe and as painful as a third degree burn. To minimize the risk of negative side effects, he would be started on a very low dose of anti-seizure medication. The dose would be gradually increased over a six-week period until he reached the recommended dose for his weight. I felt like I was poisoning my child but what choice did I have? They also recommended an MRI to make sure that there wasn't a tumor in his brain. That required putting him under anesthesia again. What a nightmare!

Jake's diagnosis of epilepsy was devastating to me. First of all, I thought, "How much can that poor child handle? He has been through enough!" Personally, I can handle having a child with a disability. I can live with the fact that I'll never have a true empty nest. I can live with the things that we can't do because of the added responsibilities associated with having a child with autism, etc. But the diagnosis of epilepsy might just be the thing to push me over the edge! I fell into a bit of depression for about two weeks. I couldn't stand the thought of eating anything, and lost a few pounds. Any loud bang in the house (signaling another possible seizure) sent me into a panic. So many scenarios were running through my mind! I was scared to be home alone with Jake. I was scared that he might have a seizure and I wouldn't be able to protect him due to his size. I was scared to take him out alone. What if he had a seizure when we were out, and fell and cracked his head open? How would I get him home? If my phone rang while Jake was at school, my heart would race fearing the worst!

I knew that I had to pull myself together. I could not and would not live like this! I made up my mind. I refused to let Jake miss out on life by keeping him in a protective bubble. I would not "punish" him for having this disorder! He deserved to continue life as he knew it, and I was going to make sure that he could. I started off by doing a lot of research and talking to the parents of other children with seizure disorders. Also, as crazy as it sounds, I watched as many YouTube videos of people experiencing grand mal seizures as I could. I had to know what to expect! I had to educate myself! When we reached his "one year seizure free " anniversary we celebrated. I'd be lying if I said that I'm completely comfortable with the situation today, but at least now I'm more focused and heading in the right direction.

Jake is a funny kid. He has been known to walk by a table in a restaurant and help himself to a french fry off of someone's plate. Once we were out to dinner at a hibachi restaurant. At the next table a woman was celebrating her birthday. The server brought her out a dessert with a candle in it. Before I could stop him, Jake ran up behind the woman and her husband, bent over between them and blew out her candle! The look on her face was priceless. Jake was quite pleased with himself! He has also been known to drop his wet bathing suit on the beach when he is finished playing in the ocean because his pockets are filled with sand. The bottom line is, sometimes he does things that the rest of us would like to do but know not to. It's pure innocence.

Jake has also become OCD as he has gotten older. Everything has to be in its place. If I put something new in his room, he puts it outside of his door. If I move his socks to a different drawer, he puts them back where they were. Also, all doors and drawers need to be closed completely. He will actually get up from a meal to close a drawer or the lid on the trashcan. According to Jake, tissues should be tucked inside of a tissue box instead of pulled through and fluffed. He once got in trouble on the school bus for getting out of his seat to put the drivers armrest down.

Jake is also very rule conscious. For example, he always turns lights off when he leaves a room. On the way home from the beach last year we stopped at a rest stop. My husband took Jake into the men's room. When they were finished, my husband walked out and Jake followed behind him. As they exited, a man from inside the rest room yelled "Hey"! Jake had turned the light off as he walked out. The problem was that someone else was still in there when the rest room went dark.

There are various challenges raising a child with autism. Something that most parents don't think about with their twenty-year old son is sending him into a men's room alone. Actually, it's one of the biggest challenges that I face when Jake and I are out in public alone. I don't like sending him into the men's room unattended. Because of the noises and sudden movements that he makes I'm afraid that someone will misconstrue his actions as something inappropriate and be unkind or even aggressive with him. He also will occasionally flush someone else's urinal while they are in the middle of using it.

Looking ahead to Jake's future concerns me the most. His intellectual deficits and innocence make him vulnerable to the evils in the world. People with autism don't have any distinctive physical attributes that would identify them as special needs individuals. Therefore, others don't have the patience or understanding with them that they would have if they realized the situation. I am hopeful that one-day Jake can live in a group home and have a supervised job; a job that will give him a sense of accomplishment. Most importantly, I pray that Jake can live a long, happy and healthy life surrounded by people who love, respect and understand him. At this point I can't even imagine not being here to love him, protect him and to ensure that he has the wonderful quality of life that he so deserves to have. However, realistically he will most likely outlive both my husband and me. Therefore, we have to make sure that a plan is in place that ensures that he has the best situation that he can possibly have. I take comfort in knowing that his sister and brother will always be there for him. They not only love him, but also have been wonderfully supportive, protective and patient with him. He could not have asked for better siblings.

Today Jake is a happy and healthy 20-year-old boy who is living his life to the fullest. As for me, I am dedicated to doing what I can to raise awareness about autism. In 2008 I was invited to help establish a charitable organization that raises money for autism awareness and research. Our group founded a non-profit organization called "The Course for the Cause". We hold annual golf tournaments and benefit dinners and have donated a substantial amount of money to Autism Speaks. This is something that I'm very proud of.

I am also a hospice volunteer. I work at an inpatient unit in addition to working as an end of life doula. I'm on call to sit with patients as they are actively dying. I want to provide whatever comfort I can while treating each patient with kindness, patience, dignity and respect. I also want their families to take comfort in knowing that their loved ones are being treated the way that they would want them to be. I hope and pray that those caring for my son in the future will feel and do the same.

So what has having a child with special needs taught me? Probably the two biggest things are patience and unconditional love.
I am more aware of the fact that everyone is someone's child. Whether that individual is disabled, mentally ill, or homeless, each human being deserves to be treated with kindness and respect. I have also come to realize that it's okay for me to be sad sometimes, or to feel exhausted, or even frustrated. These feelings don't make me a bad mother. I am human! It's okay to be human.

Heal You
by Jeanette Bambarger

Someone smiled
Someone laughed
Because of you
So you say
Now I must continue
Now I must help
But wait now
What about you?
Your smile
Your laughter
Is it in tact?
Help no one
Till you help you first
You want to light a fire?
Light your own
You want to make people happy?
Make yourself happy
This is where it must begin
Step one is with you
Each has his journey
Each has his path
If we then take care of us
Then one by one
The world will take care of itself

*H*eal yourself and you can be a guiding part of other's healing. Emphasize being a guiding strength and not doing the "work" for them. When thinking of the many life experiences I've had, one point that comes to mind is to first heal thy self. Once you've healed yourself anything is possible.

Writing something that will hopefully inspire another- that in itself is empowering and inspiring to me and I'm honored to be a part of this journey with Tammy in creating this book. Tammy and I met about a year ago and from the beginning our friendship has been one of a comfort and feeling of always having known each other. I have been a Massage Therapist, Reiki Master, been married many years and have three awesome grown kids. Healing is and has been a major part of my life. Just as I have been a guide to others in their own healing, my learned experiences from deep physical and emotional pain; loss, depression, anxiety and abuse have led me to profound healing and inner joy. Healing in any capacity can create a domino effect to then promote positivity to those around you. Without even realizing it we are helping those around us by helping ourselves. There's a lot of good that comes from your own inner peace and it will branch out to those around you as time goes on. Take your life seriously and treat it with great respect. Tell those around you how much you love them and how beautiful they are. We all need to hear these things. Don't just think about saying nice things, speak them. If you feel someone has done you wrong, learn from it and forgive them because they are worth it even if at that moment you can't see this. If in every situation and experience in our lives we practiced the true art of just accepting these as things meant to happen for our personal growth, then what an amazing place we could be in and live more peacefully. In looking into your own self you are not taking away from that of another. Actually, I see it as a major giving to all those around you because in order to heal yourself, you will need to let go, forgive, be thankful, and in the end there is always love.

Healing You Inspires Those Around You

When you can experience great fear, sadness and pain in your heart and then be able to learn to let go and move towards the opening or re-opening of the love in your heart, you want so passionately and most certainly to pass this on to others to hopefully and positively affect them. This is what I hope for you in reading my passage. Through my life's journey, thus far, putting the time and effort into ultimately healing my self has been the catapult to extreme inner peace and joy. So, if there was one thing I could inspire another to do it would be to look into you, empower you and heal you. As you heal and begin to feel better then so do others around you. To me that's a treasure because we constantly want to help others or think we need to help others around us and yet in healing ourselves we positively affect those around us. Bonus!

When you see pain in a loved one and want to heal them, show them how to do this by healing yourself. I'm not in any way promoting deserting a loved one you have concern for. My concern for you is that although we can be a source of light, encouragement and love to another, we must be careful not to lose ourselves in the process. There is everything of love to hold someone's hand and guide them through a challenging part of their journey but it is just as important to remember to be there for your self too. Otherwise, you become drained, sometimes angry, confused or anxious and I don't see how that is a guidance or healing for anyone.

Living with or having a relationship with someone that has an addiction, struggling with depression and anxiety, or anything that is so negatively affecting them, it's very hard to watch right in front of you. It's our hearts of great love that feel some of their pain. We want so much to be their rock, help them to the light at the end of the tunnel and do whatever we can think of to guide them back to a happier life. There are things you can do and you're probably already doing them. Listen to someone talk, do something fun together, or just letting one know you are there to go to that appointment they keep saying they will make. It's also nice to offer feedback on things that may have helped you in the past during your own challenging time. There are many beautiful ways to support someone who is having a tough time. We can always be there, it's just we cannot solve their problem, make them better or take away their pain.

Several years back and during a challenging time within our family I sat one day and thought…Well, I've been every kind of emotion around this person; happy, sad, empowering, empathic, kind, bought books, left notes, made appointments that they should have made on their own, and in the end the result was always the same. They were the same no matter what I did so it finally told me that I was not going to save their life because they had to be the one to want to save their life. Besides, all my efforts were really what I thought they needed or what I wanted. That's just it. It was about that person, not me. You can gladly and lovingly guide by letting them know you are there, that you love them and can even offer them some advice. In the end though, they must be the one to decide to live, to quit drinking, stop taking drugs or get help for destructive behavior. It is not our job in life to be lifesavers to others because that just drains you. If your energy is mostly directed at caring for others then where is the caring energy for you? Why not treat you with the caring and concern that you're giving out freely to others?

When we've tried everything we can think of and things remain similar then why not try something different? Be that guiding light to another showing them how to do it through your own actions. If you're feeling run down and stressed out but still putting all that energy towards someone you care for then you can fall into a kind of negative cycle, then what? So, be there still for that person but in a healthier capacity and in a more balanced way. Maybe they will follow your lead. You're not deserting someone by taking care of you. You didn't go anywhere.

People have their own journeys

Having listened to people complain about their significant other, their friend(s), their kids, the neighbors, the people they work with, the check out lady at some store, etc., what is really heard is more a complaint in our own self. There's a reason these things bothered us. All those negative feelings we allow to infiltrate us and then we give them so much unfair power. Unfair because that fear, anger, or loneliness, doesn't deserve to rent that space inside us and if we don't pay attention to it, it festers. We then feel guilt, we blame, we feel lost or abandoned-we feel bad inside.

How much of your own energy do you put towards your worries, fears and things that anger you? For example, are you worrying endlessly about the kids, the marriage, your family, friendships or your job? Guidance is one thing but constant worry and negative thought process towards others in your life is not what will be helpful to them or you. We spend significant time with concern for others because we think we know what they need. Yes, even as parents we worry way too much to the point of getting in our own way in the guidance of our own children's journey. They have mistakes to make and they must make mistakes. It is part of why we are here. One way or the other lessons have to be learned and some days, some experiences will not be pleasant. That's ok and all part of the process.

We sometimes feel this need to be in someone's business because we've decided that we know better. Then we're on this mission to save those around us. We'll change them because we have the answers and just know this is what they need, our assistance. Crazy as it may seem, parents included, we need to take a step back and really look at what we're doing and why we're doing it. Anger and fear are many times the motivators. Anger because we've been treated unfairly and might not like what's going on around us yet we choose to stay in that atmosphere. Fear of losing a loved one yet they must want to help their own self and not because you're making them change or suggest you have the answers. There are experiences that we may not agree with or understand at that moment, but in the end, each person is making the choices to where they are in this life. Many times people think if they would have or could have just done this or that, then life for this person would be better or could have been better. It's not up to you. If you want to be a guiding force in someone's healing then, again, be the guiding example in how you live your life. It doesn't mean this fixes everything around you; remember you're not here to be fixing others. Guiding and fixing are two different things. Someone wise once told me that we must go through things and not around them. Trudge right through and face things. Endless running away from or trying to cut corners when life gets challenging only makes things take so much longer to smooth out and resolve. One of the hardest things I have watched and learned is realizing that when you are watching a person you deeply care for walk towards a cliff, you will not change them and their direction unless - and this is very important - unless they decide to change. Every time, hands down. This is one of the most painful lessons and it is true.

The good thing is that as a person directs energy internally to seek healing, then things begin to change in a positive direction. All the endless yelling, frustration, 911 worry affects every aspect of a person and not in a good way. Initially when looking inward, detaching from the madness can be very painful because you have to look at it and face it. It's all necessary though because living in a constant environment of fear and stress doesn't get anyone anywhere and you find yourself waking up each day and looking at the same thing over and over again.

Change is uncomfortable because we're out of our comfort zone but give it a chance because it means you're moving past something and growing in the best way. Nothing happens overnight and when you don't know what else to think, remember there is faith.

Faith is comfort, Faith is Love, Faith is knowledge, Faith is discipline, Faith is full of integrity, Faith walks the tight rope and Faith comes out on the other side.
~Jeanette Bambarger

Ask Yourself…What's on your mind?
It's also helpful to remember that "it's not about you" from the point of realizing that others have their agenda, worries, fears and challenges yet there is a significant reason why the thing they said, their tone of voice or the way they looked at you really pushed your buttons. So that's where it's best to start.

Where is that feeling coming from? And why? How many times have we allowed something someone said or did to hurt us? We allow ourselves to feel hurt because of these things and then we hang out in that darker energy. We take the negative outbursts personal and we keep going over it in our minds to try and understand or figure out why they did something to us. What I'm trying to stress is to instead figure out why it bothers us so much. Forget that it was said or done to the point of dissecting the feelings that came over you. We are the ones who allow things and others to ruin our day or days. Put the emphasis on yourself because you are a beautiful soul that most certainly wants to be happy in this life. Life is wonderful in every kind of way if we would just allow it and truly believe in our selves. True, it's no fun, especially in the beginning, to look at things from within instead of outward but it's a priceless and huge pay off for your happiness plus it is a liberating feeling to let stuff go. It's like weight is lifted from you. Those headaches, sore shoulders and back pains need to go! My experiences with clients as a massage therapist have shown me that we all hang on to far too much.

Most people make decisions based on others and most people will disagree with this. But it's true and I know because I have done just this. I have changed my day, my thoughts, my dreams, etc., because I thought I had to do something for someone else. People think this means you're selfish to start putting the effort and energy on yourself. But wait a minute- aren't we being a little arrogant in thinking we know what the other needs? While spending all your time worrying about another you get neglected, so instead of one person being in a bad place you end up with two. It is extremely draining to be in a destructive relationship and this isn't news. So, no, you are not selfish. It shows true love for your self. If you cannot love yourself and be truthful with all of who you are then how in the world do you think you can positively affect those around you? I believe our job is not to figure out what everyone else needs but figure out what we need. As we do this we begin to heal, our light begins to shine more and we positively affect those around us by just healing us. This to me is how you guide others; be the guiding example and the rest will follow. And if they don't follow then they are to be or chose to move in another direction. That is their decision and not yours.

Our feelings guide us and this helped me immensely. I realized that it let me know where I was in life. If I was mad or felt my feelings were hurt or felt no one was listening to me, then I stopped to look at why I felt this way. That's where I started many times in looking into my own healing. Our feelings are there for a reason. They are clues to how things are going in your life. If you don't take the time to stop and ask yourself about your own feelings, then how do you think you can offer any guidance to another? It gets to be like the blind leading the blind. Feelings and thoughts are extremely important and they shape whom we are, where we are in life and also affect everyone around us as well. If you're thinking and thinking about worry, anger and sadness then that will be created around you. That way of thinking keeps us in this negative loop. Things will continue to be in the same warp until one person decides to do one thing differently and then there will be an energy shift. If, for example, you react differently or maybe don't react at all to a negative situation, then that power has nowhere to go. When we emotionally react we give destructive things power.

Think about it. If you are sad then so is your energy and so that is what you are putting out around you, around other people and all the way through to the Universe. Again, heal yourself first.

Ok, you say, well how do I do that?

Be your own project. Begin by just being present in the moment. This means realizing and understanding that there's nothing else you have to be doing. You know all those feelings of having to go here, go there, make this, do that because these are demands you have put on your self because you think you need to do these things for some other reason. Yes, this is true. When you find you are feeling rushed, stressed, worn-out (get the picture?) while doing something in your day stop right there at that moment and ask yourself why you are doing whatever it is. It's really not as complicated as it seems, I promise. Just ask yourself: Why am I feeling this way? Why am I doing this right now? Whatever it is and it can be as simple as making dinner for someone. If you're annoyed, stressed, etc., while making the dinner then-Yes, it is as simple as stopping and asking yourself why. The point is all about the feeling. Let the feeling guide you. Let the feeling inside you be a clue in your own personal treasure map. It's to help you. So you then say to yourself: Is this something that makes me happy? Am I doing this for another or me? Well, if you are doing something for another and think you must do it then you allow guilt to drive you. There is no guilt. You must then step back and see and really own this feeling for what it is. You are not doing something for you and it is not a mean or selfish thing to want to be happy. Don't you see that if you are not happy then no one around you will be either?

<u>Ok, here is an example to look at:</u>

Sally has worked all day and is tired especially since she didn't get much sleep last night. She feels worn out but feels she must get home to make dinner for the family. It's not a good feeling inside she has. In fact she thinks she might be getting sick as well but still she believes she must do all these things for her family. She rummages through the freezer and pantry and throws something together quickly and sets the table. For five minutes she feels calm while eating but then dinner with the family comes and goes quickly and she is then left to clean up the kitchen. Let's see, by now she's feeling some bitterness and possibly even resentment -feeling like she does all this stuff for her family and what do they care plus she's the one cooking and cleaning. The next thing you know it's late and she's tired and goes to bed just to believe she has to get up and do the same thing tomorrow.

Let's dissect this:

Where in this entire paragraph does it show that she has taken care of her self in any way or that she feels good, great, happy, relaxed and so on. Nowhere does it show this. There is no rule that she must make dinner, do the laundry, the cleaning, and even work at the job she has. Nope. These are all the choices that Sally made by herself. It may appear that she is supposed to do all these things but that's all that is-it "appears" this way. You want to help your kids? Then empower them. Teach them to cook, to clean and to want to open their hearts and minds to the magic of the fact that they can be and do anything they want and to not just feel that they "have to" live from some routine list of life rules.

Now it's your turn

What are you thinking about right now? Stop what you're doing, grab a notebook and write words and quick bullets of information about what's running through your brain right now. After the pen stops, wait a couple minutes and do it again. Now, look at it briefly. First, is the stuff on this list of the utmost importance? Well of course you're going to say no because there is no emergency. So, just stop. Go and listen to some nice music, your choice. Walk outside even if it's briefly and even if it's cold. Take a shower, call a friend, write down some things you're grateful for, pet your dog, watch a funny movie, draw smiley faces all over a paper, etc. Just do something that makes you smile and even if it's for a few minutes. There, you just took time for you. Keep doing this.

We are all way, way too hard on ourselves. Choose to live your dreams and keep looking ahead and choose to let go of the negative. Each one of us is unique and different things work for different people. Things that make us feel happy are personal to each individual so there is no wrong or right. Have good intention in your heart and begin doing things that make you happy. Friends may have suggestions of things to try and then begin to think on your own about little things that make you smile. It could be so simple as eating a cookie, making a paper plane, looking at comedy on a website, making cupcakes, getting your hair or nails done, reading funny cards or rearranging a room. If you're new at this, cool! You get to just start trying things! Sometimes remembering our childhood helps because that's the kind of mindset you are looking for: simple, innocent, pleasant! What things made you so happy when you were a kid? If you can't think of any or feel you don't have any, that's ok. Just think of anything that has made you smile or laugh. Start there. Also, the more intention you put into this, the more positive energy comes your way. This is so magical because new people may show up in your life and different experiences will happen all helping guide you to those positive intentions you're putting out there. Life is magical and it really is all that you decide to make it.

What calls to your heart? What moves and shakes you? What upsets you? Who gets a rise out of you? How do you feel at this very moment while reading this? Start with questions to yourself and not questions to the others around you. Our minds control everything about what's going on in our lives whether good or bad, happy or sad. It is as simple as continuous positive thinking = happier life. If you are presently living in a challenging environment then take it one day, 1 hour or even one moment at a time. You have to start somewhere. The more you really want to be happier in life and the more you believe then the faster you'll notice things change. Intention, intention and intention. Intention is a very powerful word that can change everything. Your intentions are your thoughts and just as real estate agents say that location is everything, well, our thoughts are just as important: our thoughts are everything.

Different things work for different people. Maybe you need to write positive and upbeat things about yourself on post it notes and put them all over the place. Maybe clipping pictures from magazines, pictures from the Internet of your favorite things; things that make you happy, your dreams (and with no holding back), your desires, and putting them on a bulletin board or taped on a wall may be helpful. Maybe putting positive scenes or quotes on your desktop of your computer and cell phone that you are constantly looking at will help to keep reminding your brain to shift your thoughts. Stacking a pile of uplifting books on a bookshelf that you are frequently near still means those uplifting messages and feelings are getting in your head. How about putting something pretty right inside or outside of a window in your kitchen. Placing things throughout the place you live and even your work place area that are happy to you will, again, help your brain. Get the picture now? Whatever you can do to constantly remind yourself, your brain and your thoughts to be happy, positive, relaxed, joyful, -do it!

So, you start changing the environment around you to

reflect uplifting-ness. Great! Now, at first you're not going to be a pro at this so it's important to remember that you need to be kind to yourself and give yourself a break. You will start feeling better and things will begin to change in a better direction. Energy is shifting and in the best way. When you find that you then have a bad moment or hour or even a day that is way off, do not panic. It's OK. You may have to write "It's OK" really big on a piece of paper and keep looking at to help, but my point is that it's completely normal and OK to have those yucky feelings. First of all, stuff has to come out to help you heal so allow it to come out. If you start to get down on yourself, then get into a habit of a back-up plan to help lift your spirits. All you need is to do is shift that energy instead of hovering in it. Go back to those suggestions a few paragraphs ago and here are more ideas; take a bubble bath, meditate, exercise, take a few deep breaths, sing like a rock star, chew bubble gum, etc. Do something that shifts your thinking. This helps shift you from that dark place you're in: it shifts the energy from dark towards light. The more you practice this, the better you become at catching yourself from looking at the black hole. The easier it becomes because then you'll have established a habit and once you are aware you can't go back. Your higher self will be so excited and will be elated to help you remember this so it will keep being in your face but in the best of ways and intentions!

  To find true happiness one must look inside. What gives you inner joy? I'm not referring to being married, having kids, a wonderful job, etc. I'm directing this to you and you alone. Spending some time by yourself and feeling okay with that, then you are on to something and will begin to learn more about you. This in no way is a negative to those around you and is not implying you should ignore those around you. You are a beautiful and unique soul like no other. Who are you? Begin looking inside and taking the time for you. I guarantee the happier you are with yourself, the happier people around you will be. They will feel that energy. If you want to make a difference in someone's life then be the example and without even realizing it you will positively affect those around you.

I hope in some way this has touched something wonderful deep inside you. Life is so much more then a daily routine filled with unending tasks. It's more, it's deep, and it's full of love and connection with each other. We really have all the answers inside us if we'd just take the time to listen. Take the time to listen because you are worth every moment.

I am reminded of my own beliefs, my daily attitude towards life and having the faith to move forward. There is meaning in everything and everything happens for a reason. Here are a few things to keep in mind:

>*It will be OK*
>*Family and Friends can help*
>*Pray and have Faith*
>*Life has a process*
>*All of us have, and will experience similar things*
>*You are Not alone*

* * *

My Animated Life
by Lisa Shah

A Foreword Note

I want to lay a foundational premise here. I believe in an awesome creator God, with whom I am intimately connected in oneness, and also in the laws of nature that have been set in place by this Creator.

I am convinced I came into being to live and love, to laugh and very importantly-to learn. I came to enjoy and experience many things so that I can choose to design the life I would like to live and be the co-creator of my reality. I share my life freely and quite openly so that others may know how I think about things, apply what I learn and move ever more deeply into that desired, and designed, dream life I can see for myself.

I have *so* many stories! But here and now, I am going to share a chapter my life. The story doesn't really have an ending, as I am still living my life, but you can be sure, it will suspend on a very happy note.

So, I hope you find some things to relate to and hopefully be inspired by. More than anything else, this story is about living your dreams.

We all can, you know.

Where this story begins...

Almost exactly two years ago, I was living in a perfect little beach paradise. My five children were 19-29 and all living in their own worlds. Not disconnected, but fairly self-sufficient. I had spent 2011 living in a sweet beachfront flat in Burleigh Heads Queensland, Australia, and this place was the fruition of a particular dream and very much part of my demonstration on how to work with the universal Law of Attraction and share the process with people, so they can be encouraged and inspired in their own lives.

That year, I was singing and playing piano, completing my spiritual fantasy novel and living a wonderfully artistic way of life (heaven for me! lol). I had planned a year there and then wanted to somehow get to France. Why France? Well, that is a whole other story, but it was a compelling motivation and I could see myself living a very artistic, and perhaps a somewhat gypsy-ish life there. In the mean time, I didn't really know what I wanted to do with myself, other than enjoy my beach, then, I met someone, and true to old habits, was ready to relinquish all of myself to fall into step with him.

Or was I?

He offered her the world~she said she had her own-Monique Duval

Through a sequence of events, to which I could never do justice here, I experienced intense and personally dramatic happenings such that I would never be the same again-and that's a good thing-but, as sometimes happens, there was a culminating personal event that hit my life like a ground splitting lightning strike. These things don't always *feel* good, but they can produce good, if we let them. I spent all of the latter part of 2011 coming to terms with what had taken place in the first part and in the context of my life leading up to it.

I had vowed years before that I would master the art of being comfortable in discomfort, so that I could always grow and in the preceding years I had overcome *so* many personal fears and erroneous beliefs. I wish I could go into the details here, but just to give you an idea, I had overcome alopecia, eating disorders, body image issues, fear of being alone, fear of failing, fear of lack and faced a midnight burglar (and won!). I didn't know how I'd go without some of the security blankets I'd grown accustomed to-specific routines, my own space and preventive medicines for asthma, just to name a few). I even experienced miracles and wonderful answers to prayers and learned how to do this with much more intention.

Through continuous spiritual guidance, from as back as I can remember to now, I have learned how to do all this and have progressively grown out of my inadequacies to know myself as more and more capable of handling LIFE.

Now, I am actually quite notorious for 'forcing' myself into change for the purpose of personal expansion. I started an online Masters degree as part of helping myself focus and get some grounding in my own life, and I quit the last and longest of my current music residencies, removing a large part of my income. I could have thought that through better perhaps, but it was all part of what was happening in my personal world and very much a part of my efforts to separate from 'what is'. Something in me relishes a good stretch, even as another part of me panics at the prospect of it. This time, I was going to go BIG.

I didn't want my old life anymore-and I don't mean my family or friends. I JUST WANTED MORE FROM MYSELF. I wanted to live out all the things I've tasted in my imagination...and *more*.

It's time to *fly*. I had a sense of desperation that made me feel that if I didn't do something now-maybe I never will. And seriously, in all my life **nothing** has ever been more frightening to me than the idea that I would "die with my song unsung and my vision still in my belly". That just cannot happen! France wasn't going to come to me and perhaps money and means wouldn't fall out of the sky, but I have a ton of stories about amazing and miraculous occurrences to embolden me and I knew it was time to set my intention. So, on a day in November 2011, I did.

France, May 17, 2012.

Why this date? Someone else said it, and for some reason, it resonated with me, so I embraced it.

Here's what happened...

Getting Clear on the Details

Not long after, I was talking to with my girlfriend Deborah, who had just been to France and wanted to return. She told me her birthday was May 17!! So, we decided to meet at the Eiffel Tower in Paris to celebrate her birthday. I also thought I'd go to America again and talked to a musician friend of mine I'd not seen for 25 years, who was doing music in New York, about spending the 4th of July there with him and visiting some places to sing. I also thought I'd meet other online friends I'd developed over years who were on the US east coast. I had no idea of how any of this would come about but that's ok, because I know that part is not my initial job. All I needed to do, at that point, was set the intention and start having fun, playing with the idea.

Personal Process

I was deep in an emotional process of working through all that had come up through 2011. It didn't always feel like it but I was growing stronger and more confident than I probably thought. One day, in March 2012, I decided I would not renew my lease and I would sell almost everything, keeping only my car, books, clothes and things to work with for uni (University) and very personal irreplaceable items like photos and journals. I was going to somehow practise and prepare for a nomadic French experience.

Now, you need to understand, this decision and move happened instantly. And the Sunday, two days before I had to be out of my place, someone asked if I would house sit whilst they went away camping. Two people that I'd not seen for years appeared out of my past, with trucks and boxes, to help me shift my things to a temporary place. For the next couple of months, various places and people were provided to take care of my accommodation needs and I *still* maintained my studies. I won't say that was easy to study in this upheaval, and it did cause me to reconsider the date I'd set, as the Semester ended on May 31. It made sense to make it just that little bit later, and as it turned out Deborah's plans had taken a turn, so she wouldn't be there then, either. It fit.

Provision follows vision.

The other decision I had "umm-ed and aah-ed" over was whether I would go to the United States first, or straight to France. As the months went by, more and more elements aligned for the US and didn't really open up for France. I had been to the US eight years earlier and I had lots of online connections there and some friends and even family, so I felt more comfortable launching out into that country, but even more than that, I felt that America was somehow a greater equipping for Europe. This trip was a learning process all the way and I believe we are always growing up into the next set of boots, so to speak. I knew I would feel so much more confident to travel further after a successful stint in the US.

The Best Advice

One of the very best bits of mothering advice I've ever given my children, or anyone, (including me!) is...

"Take only the ways that are firm."(from Proverbs 4:26)

When it comes to making decisions, this is priceless. Don't do something that feels shaky. If you know why it feels shaky and you can address it so that it feels sound, sure, go ahead. Otherwise, wait. If you absolutely *must* make a decision, then consider your options, make your choice and *make it the right choice.* Do it wholeheartedly. Commit to it. Don't second-guess yourself, because, here's the thing:

It is actually the wholehearted element that makes it work.

You will know if/when it ever feels right to change it. It will feel sure. Just like me changing my dates. It's something of a paradox to commit to something and yet still understand the flexibility of being open to modifications. This is a fundamental and crucial, yet little appreciated life skill. But, if you want to live like I do- attuned to ebbs and ready to flow with great opportunities, yet be safe –it's entirely essential.

Take only the ways that are firm.

Commit to Your Intention

So, I decided I would head directly for New York, drop in on Neville, sing a song or two, then head down to my friends in Maryland. I had set the middle of April as the due date for making this decision between France and the US. I still had no work, was living on a student allowance and did not know how the ticket to fly would come. I just stayed focussed on the plan to leave the country on May 31 and I looked for ways to cultivate the 'state of being' that was aligned with that and was practising any and all the various techniques I knew to help with this. I *had* to leave the country. I *had* to get out of the known.

The other thing was that I really wanted to go to Sydney and visit my family before I left. I didn't know when I would be back, so I wanted to see my siblings, parents, other children and extended relatives. We have annual reunions, so we're all quite connected and the only really block to this was once again, the money to fly.

But just 'wanting' isn't enough. The 'want to' has to be big enough to draw a committed intention. Everyone has heard the saying *Where there is a will, there is a way!* That's the truth. If you are really determined, nothing short of death will stop you, and perhaps not even that.

As W.H.. Murray said

"Until one is committed, there is hesitancy, the chance to draw back. Concerning all acts of initiative (and creation), there is one elementary truth, the ignorance of which kills countless ideas and splendid plans: that the moment one definitely commits oneself, then Providence moves too. All sorts of things occur to help one that would never otherwise have occurred. A whole stream of events issues from the decision, raising in one's favour

all manner of unforeseen incidents and meetings and material assistance, which no man could have dreamed would have come his way. Whatever you can do, or dream you can do, begin it. Boldness has genius, power, and magic in it. Begin it now."

from the Scottish Himalaya Expedition 1951

From Wanting to Having-Live Like You mean It

One night, at the beginning of May, I was thinking about what I could do to help shift whatever might be in the way of me receiving what I wanted and I asked myself, are you actually ready to go? Right now? It was then I realised there were actually still a number of 'to dos' to address, such as visa matters, my belongings and shifting them out of a friend's shed and into storage, what to do with my car and insurance options for travel. No! I wasn't ready for my ticket and I know this was part of not being convinced of leaving and was causing a stalemate in the energy.

I decided to do anything that I *could* do. At the same time, I was keeping a kind of documentation and running a campaign to share my journey with others. I had integrated it into my degree and was incorporating the world of Social Media as a major player in being able to fulfil personal dreams on a global scale, for anyone. This meant I was planning a musical event, singing and playing and keyed it up with a local recording studio, a connection which also came through Social Media, namely Facebook.

I kept people informed with what was happening on this "Gratitude and Agapé Love" tour. I had been blogging where I was staying and what I was up to since leaving my fixed address. A great deal of the information is viewable on You Tube, Facebook and my own website, Lisa Shah Escape.

With a Little Help From My Friends

Another friend of mine, who was experiencing a rather nasty divorce started spending some time with me and helped with so many practical things and was wonderful company to boot.

God uses people. The universe is geared to work through the existing channels-on the most part, anyway. One connection leads to another which leads to an opportunity and all kinds of wonderful blessings arise- and *all* out of the committed decisions we make. True faith requires no contrived broadcasting, but trusts. It doesn't mean provision can't come via word of mouth, and it often does, but it just isn't done to have that coercive agenda and call it 'faith in God'.

So, the countdown to the day of departure drew nearer and I focussed on doing all that was in my hand to do to keep the energy moving, staying in the place of peace and joy. I would browse flight info and insurance options and think about what I would be doing in the US.

I 'constructed' Photoshop images of me with my online friends, visiting places like Washington and being in NYC for Independence Day. I also envisaged singing and speaking in various places and mocked up my own visual and verbal versions of these. I call this process "Fabricating Memories". This is one of my favourite Life Creating activities and I had already experienced so much success with it that I trusted it to help me create this adventure.

Role-playing is an effective tool, so if you find a way to play-act your desires, you may find they come to fruition very quickly. In an effort to simulate the reality of having my tickets and my trip to Sydney, I browsed some sites and found and purchased flights to the US. To my amazement they were processed and for about a week, I had actual flights booked!

This worked, for by the time the 'hold' was due to expire, someone made a donation of $1000 on my site via Pay pal and, combined with other means I'd attracted that week, I was able to buy the tickets I had intended to get all along. I felt encouraged and went ahead and booked my Sydney flights in confidence, only to discover that I had the money to cover them too because they had an *exceptional sale right then.*

My friend bought my PA (musical equipment) off me and that gave me $600 in my pocket, and I still had a student allowance until the end of June, which was enough to cover certain home obligations that continued. I was determined to return to a different life when I did finally come back, so I let it go without any regret.

So, just two weeks prior to leaving, I finally have my flights booked including insurance and a $13 bus ride from NYC to Baltimore. And guess what day I left?

May 31.

On Reflection

So, the combination of taking *joyful* action where I could by going ahead with my farewell gathering plans, visa issues, researching itineraries, documenting the process in 'fabricated memories' and regular updates all worked to help me keep my fun energetic focus on my desired outcome-and that's what allowed it all to come into fruition.

The Next Stage

My university semester also finished on May 31 and I left with a final project yet to be completed and get submitted. With time zone changes and a full 24 hours of travel, it was in late, but do you think I minded so much by then? Real life happening to you is just so much bigger than theorising about it in some kind of paper. I, very wisely, deferred for next year. I simply wanted to engage in this adventure, blog it and document it candidly and then assemble it later when I resumed, for the project I had proposed that integrated my travels.

I landed in NYC and caught the Airport and A- and PATH trains (Yes, I caught the legendary "A-train"!) to cross the Hudson where I met up with my bass player friend from my teens. It was such a cool experience! He had a little two bedroom flat right above Grove St station. In the following weeks, I experienced Washington DC in summer, saw many memorials and a few parts of the Smithsonian Museum, fulfilling a number of my *fabricate memories*. Union Station is amazing! I stayed in beautiful places, where wild deer peered in my window and I had a lovely personal space and made wonderful friends. I was featured on a Philadelphian radio broadcast, and a 30-minute cable TV interview in Maryland, as well as sang in a Country Club and spoke for the entrepreneurial network for which I'd written the theme song.

From Hoboken, I watched an orange moon rise behind the 4th of July Fireworks over the Hudson and I sang with renowned musicians at the Open Mic nights at *The Bitter End* and *The Village Underground*. (An Open Mic is where anyone can come, put their name on the list and have their turn at performing. It took some courage for me because although I was used to performing on my terms, this was music on a raw and real level I hadn't done for some time. Man! It felt so good to reclaim this aspect of myself!) I met some of my most precious online and earliest Facebook friends and made some lovely memories with new ones, and after 5-6 weeks on the East Coast, I flew into the sunset for a scheduled 3 ½ week visit with other friends and to see my older sister in the San Francisco Bay Area, California.

The Next Stage

I landed in California on July 10, and really, I just wanted to go straight back to NYC. I had such a wonderful time there and wanted to see more. I left with a plan to come back and sing again with the guys on August 6.

Aside from speaking at a Successful Thinkers meeting on August 2 and seeing my sister for a little while, I really didn't know what I was going to do. I kept thinking that there was a 'space' for something that I obviously didn't know about yet, but I was curious. Also, although everything I needed was taken care of to date, I was a bit disappointed that I hadn't somehow figured out how to be rich yet. That may sound funny, but I really felt this endeavour was very much about coming into the life of my dreams, getting beyond the mentality of lack forever and establishing myself in some way that would allow me to contribute in so many more ways.

Although, I didn't suddenly get rich, I did have valuable moments of insight and realised that contribution was at the heart of my wanting to be able to generate income. I want to be...no, I AM a wealthy philanthropist. I have a wealth of ability, talents and various giftings and whether I had finance manifesting or not, I certainly had plenty of wealth out of which to begin to bless the planet and its inhabitants.

This thinking put my focus back on my novel and another anecdotal book I'd written on self-awareness. They needed to be in a form that I could get into the hands of people so they could be the light they were designed to be. I'd begun the process but hadn't completed it, so right there, whilst staying with incredibly precious friends in Alameda, California, I completed the work required to get both these works published. Any money needed to do so was already paid, I had just not committed.

So, I committed.

Both books were live by that August. One, online as an e-book, the other as a hard copy novel.

A Little Work and A Little Play

While still staying with these great people, I visited Santa Cruz and had some wonderful fun with cable cars and visiting Pier 39 in San Francisco. My sister, knowing how much I wanted to revisit Sausalito, had taken me there straight from the airport. That was another very strong desire fulfilled. I had a few days with my sister and nieces before moving down to Alameda, but more significant moments were to come.

After discovering the fun and potential of Open Mics from my time in New York, I was all fired up to find the local places and start singing! I started at the Washington Inn on 10th Avenue, playing their grand piano whilst waiting to meet my friend for the first time, in person, and being introduced to Successful Thinkers in Foster City. (A business networking function). I attended a number of these, thanks to the grace and generosity of my friend and it was through one of the other attendees we heard of nearby venues where I could sing.

The first one was perfect! The house band was a jazz ensemble and they backed me as my friends videoed it. Yes, it's still up on You tube ☺

But it was the Open Mic the following week that really altered the direction of my life.

Creating a Dream Reality Using Animation

A couple of months earlier, as part of a drawing project for Uni, I had created a really sweet animation. It featured two little stick figure characters that had quite distinct appearances. The male was black with a white goatee and the girl darkhaired and happy with a red bow and frilly skirt.

They appeared against a watercolour backdrop I had copied from a Lloyd Rees artwork of Venice (another assignment). These little characters could literally remove their hearts and place another in the space. This pair saw each other from opposite sides of a Venetian waterway and wanted to exchange hearts. They travelled back to a bridge, where they met in the middle and swapped them, carefully placing each one within the cavity of the other.

They ran down the far side, boarded a gondola and took off down the river, just as a very religious character in black came down to stop them. He was carrying a picket sign that said "LAW" and had a 'no heart swapping' graphic on the flipside. But it was too late. You can view this little piece here.

https://www.youtube.com/watch?v=kc0X8kiGA8s

I took some time creating their names and back-stories. I knew the female was a representation of me but I wanted a name like "John the good", or "Robert the Brave" or "Larry the Lover", or something for the male. I finished this a couple of months earlier, put it to a song my daughter Sarah wrote and recorded and I just loved it. It made me smile.

So, we'd heard of another Open Mic, very nearby which was happening on the following Wednesday the 24th of July (24/7), so, after playing the piano all afternoon down at the Washington Inn on 10th Av in Oakland, my friend and I decided to put my name on the list at the venue. We walked in at about 7:00. This is a bar, not a restaurant, so we asked for the list and I put my name at the top (we wanted to get in early! lol) and then, we went and ate dinner a block away, where I had sung the week before. We considered not going back, but the staff who served us dinner recommended we go and that the music is good, so we went back.

As we walked in, the house band was setting up in the back. Something shiny flashed and drew my attention. It was the Ankh earring of a very cool looking guy. According to Larrie, he'd already seen me. And I believed him, because that minute, when I first saw him, must have been the only time he wasn't staring at me! My friend and I sat down and as he continued to set up and talk about "expressing your individuality" and putting your name on the list. I wanted to retain some measure of 'cool', so didn't want to say I'd come in an 90mins earlier and put myself right at the top! Larrie just kept looking at me.

"Do I look like a singer, or something?" I asked my friend. "That guy won't stop staring at me!"

So, they opened the night and another performer, who had brought a keyboard in, started playing. Larrie came straight to me and asked me if I wanted to be on his list. In the end, I blurted out,

"What makes you think I'm not already on your list?"

Of course, he heard my accent then. My goodness!

"So, what you wanna sing?" he asked enthusiastically.

"That depends...am I playing, or you?"

"You play??"

"Yes. Can I do originals or do I have to do covers?"

"You write too???"

Man! He was beside himself. It was irresistible. *He* was irresistible!

"Do you think that guy would let me play his keyboard?"

"Well, He'd be a fool to tell you 'no'!"

And that's how it got started. My turn came up very soon after that, Jon Otis, who played congas accompanied me as I presented my two originals. Larrie insisted then that he sing a song with me too, so we did *Will You still Love Me Tomorrow*...with an impromptu modulation from Larrie. It went off!

He called me "baby" and I was gone.

To hear Larrie tell our story, he says, "Cupid hit me in the head with a baseball bat!"

So, we enjoyed the evening together. I left around 1 am and I realised I hadn't got any details but this man's name Larrie Noble Sr. But as he is listed as Larrie Noble Sr. with *his middle name*, on Facebook, I couldn't find him. At about 2 am, I got a call.

It was Larrie!

After I left, he found my red music book. :) It was like Cinderella leaving her glass slipper. I felt a little exposed, actually. That book had originals in it and for another musician to read it, felt like my diary was open!

"Now, I have to see you again." He said. :)

It's been 20 months since we met and we have been pretty much inseparable since then. Even across more than 7100 miles of ocean. He has visited me in my home and met my family and I am once again in Alameda as I write.

Larrie [the] Noble Sr., with his dark skin and white goatee, who gave me his heart, and to whom I have given mine.

It's far from being the end of any story (and I skipped so many in the telling!), we are making plans together to record the songs we've been writing for each other under the name of *Our Fireside Romance* (because we met at *The Fireside Lounge*). We are setting our sights on France. Along the way, we just keep creating beautiful moments that become golden memories-and we share them freely with our friends online, just as we always have.

A Final Comment...for Now

This story is about how we can, by being brave and decisive, create a life of magic, adventure, love and dreams fulfilled. There is so much more to share than the little that's here, but I hope it's enough to inspire even just a single reader to launch out into the beautiful sea that is their BIGGER life.

With great love, this I pray.

* * *

Transformational Love
by Lynn Molnar

> ...I may understand all secrets and know everything there is to know, and I may have faith so great that I can move mountains. But even with all this, if I don't have love, I am nothing. I may give away everything I have to help others, and I may even give my body as an offering to be burned. But I gain nothing by doing all this if I don't have love. Love is patient and kind. Love is not jealous, it does not brag, and it is not proud. Love is not rude, it is not selfish, and it cannot be made angry easily. Love does not remember wrongs done against it. Love is never happy when others do wrong, but it is always happy with the truth. Love never gives up on people. It never stops trusting, never loses hope, and never quits.
>
> *(1 Corinthians 13:2-7 ERV)*

Does everyone deserve love? What happens if you refuse to love? Is it possible to fail at love? Is there a lonely side to love? What if you miss your chance to love?

Have you ever experienced meeting someone for the first time, and you know instantly they will be an important person in your life? I met such a person on the first day of high school. We met when I walked into my second class of the day, English 101 taught by Mrs. Stigliano. I saw him sitting in the front row, second seat and was immediately drawn to him and wanted to catch his attention. I walked past him and took a seat, third row, third seat, but he did not see me. I thought to myself I needed to do something so that he would notice me, so I got up and sharpened my pencil. As I walked back to my seat he still didn't notice me, so I stared down at my desk in defeat. It was then I saw a hand reach across my desk. I looked up and that's when our eyes met! It was him! He leaned over and said, "You didn't have to sharpen your pencil to get my attention, it only prolonged our meeting." I was smitten with a young man named C.J. McDermott. I watched him from my seat two rows back from that day until the end of the school year. I watched him from Shakespeare to George Orwell and all through vocabulary lessons. I thought I was only an observer, but actually I was a full participant in love.

I learned a lot that year in English class, not just academic. But about half way through the school year, Mrs. Stigliano cautioned us with a great admonition. As she stood in front of the class, purposely making eye contact with each student, she warned, "Look around...not all the people in this room will be with you on graduation day. Not because they dropped out, but because they died. Look around the room, and ask yourself, who will be missing."

I gazed around the room and looked at my classmates. I was still situated in the middle of the room, so I was able to see C.J. and several other of my friends. I went row by row, seat by seat, calculating the value of life like some mathematical equation until I came to C.J. Then I stopped calculating. I begged God, "Take anyone, take me, but don't take C.J."

Curious how life is...about two years later, my darkest fear would become reality.

It was a Saturday night, no different than any other in my teenage life. I had just watched television with my mother and went to bed. It was only about 8:30pm, but that night I was unexplainably tired and somber. Somehow my unconscious knew something was wrong. Several times during my sleep I would awake gasping for breath, frightened to the core from the nightmares that had just consumed me.

One of the nightmares began with me learning how to drive for the first time. I was excited to gain this new responsibility but yet overwhelmed with the power that I now wielded control over a two ton vehicle. I marveled at how such a small thing as the steering wheel was so easily manipulated, with only a slip of the hand this machine could alter lives forever. In the dream I was behind the wheel, sitting tall and trying to be mature and calm. Not easy for this sixteen year old girl, especially because her driving instructor was also her gym teacher. He stood 6 feet 4 inches tall and was not once ever seen smiling.

In my dream, I was driving on a smooth road, and everything was fine until I ran over a squirrel. I felt the little bump as the car went over his little body. As the dream progressed, I ran over a cat, the car jostled with a larger bump, and my driving instructor demanded me to keep going. With tears in my eyes and trembling hands at the wheel, I drove forward, then I ran over a dog. The bump was so huge that the car shimmied and jostled to get over the dog, I felt the force of the car as it squished the dog, I heard the crunch of his body, and then the boom as the tires returned to the pavement. Terrified and nearly hysterical, my instructor demanded me to continue on driving. The next bump was a human and the raw emotion for what was about to happen caused me to awake gasping for air and trembling. I remember looking around the room to determine if what I had just experienced was reality. I saw the glowing digital clock, it read almost 10:00pm. I saw the family dog, Lady, sleeping peacefully and it was her stillness that assured me that it was just a horrible nightmare. I will never forget the nightmares I experienced that night. I didn't understand what was happening until I went to school on Monday.

I was one of thirty or so teens gathering in homeroom for an attendance check to start the day. My friend, Colleen shared with me that C.J. was killed by a drunk driver in a hit and run accident 9:30 Saturday night. In that instant, I remembered my nightmare. In that instant, I felt no pain, just pure numbness. I tried to listen to everything else she was saying, but I could no longer hear her, as if I had just been sucked up by a vacuum and I was being pulled away from reality. A few minutes went by and I watched in a daze as everyone else left the room to go to their first class. I was too stunned to move. I stood there in disbelief until the loud ringing of the school bell startled me back to reality.

Over the next few months, I became very depressed and withdrawn. I wore the same clothes almost every day, stopped doing my homework, cried from sun up to sun down and refused to eat anything that was once living. I was waiting to die. I even considered suicide. I counted out the number of days after C.J.'s last birthday that he died, and then calculated my own death to be the same number of days after my next birthday, 101 days. I wanted to be with C.J. more than I wanted to be alive. My heart was wounded and confused and nothing brought me comfort or solace. I once again could not understand the formula for which life is calculated. What is the value of life? What determines value? I was taught that no one dies without fulfilling their purpose for living. How could it be that I was still alive and he was not? I felt guilty that I was still alive.

Another month had gone by, and I was still waiting to die. One evening while I was trying to find a radio station I stumbled across a church program being broadcasted on the radio. I don't recall anything the preacher said on that particular broadcast, but I remember after the program ended I got down on my knees at the foot of my bed. It was here I reached an agreement with God. I admitted to God that I did not understand the formula for life. I could not comprehend how He calculated value and purpose, but that I trusted Him, because He was God and omniscient. I decided that night that as long as I am still living, then God must have a purpose for me, and I would spend the rest of my life in pursuit of that purpose.

From that evening forward, I would no longer try to understand the formula for life, but rather begin living life. The tragedy of losing love caused me to see myself in a new perspective. Life was teaching me about love and the depth of sorrow it can bring. It was one year after C.J.'s death that I was asked to write his memoriam for our high school yearbook.

The Clock Still Moves

One day two strangers met
And they quickly formed a circle
A circle filled with adventure and laughter

That circle soon closed
And the two strangers had created a friendship
A friendship that would stand the test of time

So the two strangers continued to walk together
Loving life and sharing secrets
All within this closed circle

But soon this circle broke
And one of the strangers went away
Too soon for the one left behind

After the circle was broken, the stranger left behind
Was scared of life and of the future
So he closed the circle again

But the circle was dark
And the one left behind
Was safe, but didn't understand why

So the stranger left the circle
And found that there was never
Just one circle in the other stranger's life

And in these other circles
The stranger left behind
Found the strength to live

So life for the one left behind, continued
Continued with the memory
Of the one who went away

And now, the memories are easier to recall
The friendship is still there
But the pain is not

And as I look upon
That empty chair of yours
I pray that you can see me

I pray that you can approve of me
Then, now, and in the future
I pray that you can be proud of me, always

You are my past
You know my future
You are the part of me that makes me whole

And I love you dearly for that.

Life did not end for me on the day C.J. died, nor did it end for C.J. He is in heaven and we will be reunited just as soon as my purpose is fulfilled. C.J.'s mother raised him in the Catholic faith, and during his youth, he studied the Bible and was an Altar Boy. C.J. made peace with God long before I even knew I had to. C.J. was my first guide in life, and many years after his death, he still inspires me to keep searching out my purpose. Sometimes I get preoccupied with other things, that I forget that I even have a purpose. I forget we all have a purpose in life.

An encounter with love can be brief, but last a whole lifetime. I have lived more of my life without C.J. than with him, but that is the power and inexhaustible reach of love. When we are touched by pure unconditional love, we are forever changed. Sometimes we search out that love, while other times it reaches out for you.

Several years ago I was working at a local university. This school had an open pet policy, meaning I was able to take my new puppy, Hero, a six month old golden retriever to work with me every day. Being able to have Hero at work enabled me to meet people I would not ordinarily meet, especially those who were hurting in private.

A dog is able to communicate unconditional love to a human. A dog allows people who are complete strangers to embrace them, to cry on their shoulders, without one ounce of judgment. A dog looks at you with compassion and understanding that touches your very soul. I have seen students stop, fall on their knees and weep with their arms around Hero. I have witnessed bedridden elderly people rise up their frail bodies just to touch Hero's ears. Their eyes would spark with enthusiasm and unabated joy like Christmas morning, all just to touch a dog.

During one of our lunchtime walks, Hero was drawn to a woman sitting on a park bench. He sat down right in front of her. I tried to get him to move because I could tell she was praying and very upset. I didn't want to disturb her, but Hero would not budge and he waited for her. When his big brown eyes met her tear stained eyes, she exclaimed, "I do believe. I know you heard me!" She went on to share with me that she is in the midst of a tremendous crisis. She thought God might be angry with her because she hasn't always done the right thing. She was asking God if He still loved her and to send her a sign that He does. That's when she opened her eyes and saw Hero sitting in front of her. She knew that only God could cause a dog to sit in front of her like that! She experienced the realness of God's love through the eyes of a dog.

That event, and many others like that helped me love again. I didn't realize that I had quarantined myself from love. For the first time in decades I was allowing myself to be loved by a big red dog, named Hero. I began to experience for myself that a dog's love is a drop in the bucket compared to the depth of love that God has for us. I began to see how desperate people are for kindness, for compassion, and how desperate I had become too.

Life has a way of wearing us out. As an adult I found myself distracted from my teenage ambitions. Over time, I had rationalized my aspirations as misguided youthful energy and even forgot who I was along the way. But thankfully, when we commit our hearts and all our dreams to God, He doesn't forget. He will bring it to pass at the correct time. God will never stop reaching out to us. God will never give up on us, and He will always love us. And if we forget, may we be reminded when we see a dog. This is why I started a non-profit charity called Thankful Paws. People need love and to be accepted for who they are, right now. The love that a dog offers not only embraces, but empowers us with a sense of belonging. Through Thankful Paws, we are able to celebrate the bond between pet and companion. We help people keep their pets which motivates them to love, to share love and to find hope even when all else looks bleak.

A few years ago, I learned of a lady who was living out of her car with her cat. She had to find a new home for her cat because summer was coming, and she can't keep her cat in a hot car all summer. She was doing the best she could, working two jobs, but financially difficult times were unavoidable for her. She didn't want her cat to suffer, she thought of the well-being of her cat before her own. She didn't mind making the sacrifice because she loved and received the love of her cat. They accepted each other and it didn't matter where they lived, as long as they were together.

Stories like this were finding their way to me on a regular basis, until I became one of those stories. I was finishing up my college degree, when a mistake in the financial aid office caused me to lose my financial aid award. I had five courses to complete until graduation, and now, I was no longer able to take classes. I suddenly owed the school thousands of dollars and a few months to pay the tuition bill if I wanted to graduate. So, little by little, I emptied out my apartment by donating my belongings to Goodwill. I moved from a two bedroom apartment in the county to renting a 200 square foot studio in the city. I made it through by cutting costs, and working three jobs while taking classes at another university. That level of work and stress is not sustainable. Fortunately for me, I was able to do it, but unfortunately for many people that is the condition of their life.

There are so many people living in such volatile circumstances, struggling to pay their bills, to keep a roof over their heads. Everyone's stress levels are exacerbated.

Unfortunately, some people panic and decide to abandon or put down their faithful pet. They lose sight of the love and focus on the numbers, they are trying to solve the equation of life. I learned the story of one young man who did panic. He was a young college graduate, trying to find a job. He had an apartment and a yellow lab. He wasn't able to find a job, so he was evicted from his apartment. There was no place for him to go, so he became homeless. After a while of living on the streets, he became more and more depressed. One day he decided that he was an unfit parent to his dog, and he didn't want his dog to suffer and be homeless, so he shot and killed his dog. He thought that was the right thing to do. A few hours later, so completely overwhelmed with grief that he killed his best friend, he turned the gun on himself. His suicide note said that he couldn't live with what he had done, and there were no other options for him. I think of this young man often and hope through Thankful Paws we are able to prevent another such tragedy.

Thankful Paws is a food bank for pets. Its purpose is to help those who are struggling financially keep their pets. At some point, we all try to calculate the value of life. We wonder if our life has meaning and purpose. We wonder if God hears our prayers. There are so many times when we are weary of fighting the financial fight, we lose sight of ourselves. We lose sight of hope. We begin to make wrong assumptions about who we are and what the future will be like. Some think that surrendering their pet is the right thing to do. We struggle with what it means to be responsible. We begin to question what love is. We wonder if love is irresponsible.

Imagine for a moment, you have your dog or cat with you, and life is good. You and your pet live with plenty to eat and a nice home. However, lately, there have been rumors about layoffs at work, and with each passing day you get nervous about your job. You are worried about losing your home, and what will the future be like? Then, it happens, you get notice that in two weeks, you will not have a job. As time goes by, you have been trying to get a job and get assistance, but the landlord wants his rent, and you don't have it. You scrimp and pawn everything you own just to keep your home. You want to keep your pet, and do everything you can but you are scared, and have no one to turn to.

What do you do?

You decide one day that you will get up and close the door to your home, with your pet inside, for the last time. You hope and pray that someone kind and loving finds your beloved pet, and that your pet will understand why you abandoned him. You roll the dice on a fifty-fifty chance that your pet will not be sent to the local kill shelter. The other option is that you close the door to your home with your pet in your arms. You roll the dice and struggle to stay together while living on the streets. You try to get assistance, perhaps stay at a shelter while your dog stays outside, but you worry - what if someone takes your dog? You discover that you can't leave your dog outside. You discover that most people look at you with disgust and shame.

They look at you like a failure, sometimes yelling at you, sometimes cursing at you that you are worthless. You want to tell them that only a few months ago, you were working in an office and that you even graduated college. But no one will listen to you. Soon, you discover, there are few to no shelters that help people with pets. It is either abandon your pet, and come inside or stay outside living in a park. There is nothing in between.

This scenario plays out every day across America. Recently, I was told of a young family with such a plight. A young man who had a six year old dog that he raised from a puppy. He then began dating a young lady, got married and had a baby. They were living modest, but happy, until he got laid off from his construction job. Without any income, they lost their apartment. Because of the baby, they were able to get assistance quickly and a place to stay, but because he had the dog, he was not allowed to take the dog where his family was staying. For a while, he kept the dog in their car, even sometimes slept with the dog outside in the car, choosing to care for his first family member too. One night, he and the dog went to visit his wife and baby, but a neighbor afraid of dogs complained. The whole family was kicked out. Now everyone is sleeping in the car.

Is that what love looks like? Is that being responsible or irresponsible? Does that dog deserve love? Does that family deserve love? Does the person who complained deserve love? It is not for us to judge what other people do. How many of us have friends and family members who really questioned our decisions? You know how it feels to be questioned for doing what you believe is right. You have felt the sting of accusation and judgment. Why do we then, inflict it on a complete stranger? Who deserves your love? Who deserves your time? Who deserves your judgments? Recently through Thankful Paws, we helped a lady who escaped a domestic abuse situation. She fled from another state and came with her baby and her dog. I am not sure how she found us, but her bravery motivates and propels me to believe in the work of Thankful Paws. Again, here was a lady risking it all to protect not just her child but also her dog. It would have been easier for her to leave the dog behind, but she knew if she left the dog, he would be abused and beaten to death. There are few provisions for people who are escaping abusive relationships with pets. What would you do? Did you ever have a childhood dream? Have you asked yourself recently, what is my goal in life? Is this the direction I want my life to continue? Do I love without fear? Do I allow myself to be loved? Did I stop loving under the guise of protecting myself?

As a child, my pets were of paramount importance to me. I valued them as if they were my real family. Looking back, I see that I accepted the love of a pet and it was a buffer from the realities of the world in which I lived. I remember sharing ice cream cones with my dog, running along the beach getting all sandy and wet with my dog. The best part of the day was curling up in bed with my best friend, knowing he would watch over me at night and be there when I first opened my eyes in the morning. However, today many children don't get to experience those magical moments. A child who doesn't learn how to treat a pet, how to love a pet or how to receive the love of a pet, will be less likely to understand what unconditional love is all about. Many times, my dog, Hero and I are approached by children, some of them know how to pet a dog, while others have thrown rocks and sticks. Instead of yelling at the children, I try to teach them how to approach a dog, to pet him and how to respect a dog.

I grew up at the beach and I can remember from my earliest memories, my mother teaching me to respect the ocean. The ocean is beautiful, the ocean is a place of reflection and solitude but it is also powerful. She warned me that the same thing that I love and admire, can kill me, and that I needed to respect the ocean. As a child, I did not fully understand what my mother meant. As I matured, I began to understand the lesson she was trying to teach me, and I am thankful for such a wonderful mother. She instilled in me a love for animals, a love for kindness tempered with respect. She is a great mother whom I love and honor. She was right by teaching me as a child to respect the ocean and to respect animals. Pets are like children, they are born dependent on us, but unlike most children, pets remain dependent. Pets innately respect us and love us for being human, they don't ask us to prove love, they just accept it.

I always find it peculiar that we ask of each other to be 'humane' but in reality it is asking us to be more pet like. We never see another dog attack another dog just for fun. An orange cat would never plot genocide on black cats. A dog would never put a cat in a microwave just to see what would happen. It is people that do these horrific things. It is people who were once children and lost their empathy for others.

Today's children, and today's society need empathy more than ever before. There is so much compassion that is lacking, too much respect is lost for our fellow man. Some children grow up having cyber-pets, a virtual reality dog or cat. No physical bond, no puppy breath, no kitten's mew. In fact, if a child forgets to walk or feed the cyber dog there are no real implications. If the dog dies, they just re-boot and get another. No personal contact, no direct emotional connection. This is so sad! We can be an impetus for changing that! We can love! We can show love every day!

The way you love your pet is not a solitary event. Even if you never considered it before, people are observing how you interact with your pet. They may never tell you but perhaps because you kindly walk your dog, and pick up after him, you have inspired compassion in another. I believe kindness has a ripple effect. Let us be the first to throw the stone, not in judgment, not in accusations, but in kindness. Throw the stone of forgiveness, throw the stone of love and watch the ripple effect! We never know how far a dream will lead us. We never know how a stranger's life will impact us. People and pets come into our lives for a season. Some we wish stayed longer, but only God holds time in His hands. The choice is ours how we live. We can chose to live like a dog, never harboring hatred, forgiving and forgetting, living in the moment. Conversely, we can chose to live begrudgingly, and with each passing year close our hearts to unconditional love. God is the author of

unconditional love, it is only through Him that we have the ability to love. Pets bring out that love in our hearts. Let us not be afraid to share love with others. Dogs never miss an opportunity to wag their tails, let's celebrate the friends and welcome the strangers in our lives. We never know when transformational love will enter our lives.

One of Hero's favorite things to do is jump in a pond to fetch a ball. When he hits the water, he has a huge ripple effect. Hero has inspired me to leave a ripple effect too, not just in the pond, but in life. If you are interested in learning more about Thankful Paws, or starting a pet charity in your area, please feel free to contact me through our website, www.thankfulpaws.org. A portion of the proceeds of this book is donated to Thankful Paws. Donated to Thankful Paws.

* * *

Happy or Grateful
by Buddy Teaser

We do a lot of things at Soles4Souls but the most important is fighting poverty by distributing new and used shoes and clothes while helping to lessen the environmental impact of the four billion pounds of textiles (footwear and apparel) we put into landfills each year in the US. For example, since Soles4Souls started in early 2006, we have distributed more than 25 million pairs of shoes and millions of pieces of clothing. Which means that by collecting new and used shoes and clothes we kept almost 30 million pounds of textiles and shoes out of landfills. More importantly, we put them to good use by getting them on the feet and backs of people who need help.

One of the questions I spend a lot of time thinking about related to our work is- are we Happy or Grateful? How are those two feelings related? And for someone leading an organization dedicated to fighting poverty isn't that an odd question anyway?

Before I started as the CEO at Soles4Souls, I probably would have felt that way. But now, just about two years into it, my sense is that it is probably the most important question we have before us.

Last year, I read a piece by the president of the American Enterprise Institute, Dr. Arthur Brooks. He wrote at length about what makes people happy. Based on the hundreds of comments following the opinion piece, there are a lot of people who want to argue about the meaning of the four values he focuses on: faith, family, community and work. There are just as many who want to argue about how much of our happiness comes from genetics and one time events – both of which play a significant role in how satisfied we are with our lives…but not as much as you might think, which I'll come back to.

The part that really caught my attention, however, is around work and the impact that it has on happiness. Speaking personally, my work at Soles4Souls is the most rewarding thing I've ever done in my life. I have never been happier. I see a similar spirit in our employees, our volunteers and our donors. It's a virtuous circle being around others who derive happiness from what they do at work every day. As I like to say, it's work that matters.

I also see this in lives of the individuals, mostly women, with whom we work in our microenterprise program. We help them create their own jobs in developing countries, by selling shoes in their local markets. Often, they are working to get out of devastating poverty – a type of poverty most of the people reading this book have never experienced. Research shows that while money doesn't buy happiness after a certain point, these women are a long way from that worry. But I do know, from talking with them and our partners, that having real work to do is almost as important as the income generated. To quote from Dr. Brooks, "… the secret to happiness through work is earned success."

However, Haiti, where Soles4Souls does a lot of microenterprise work, is a place that doesn't often foster a feeling of success. Though people work hard every day to just stay alive, it doesn't often seem like happiness is part of the mix.

Here are some grim statistics for a little context:

- 78% of Haitians are poor and living on less than US$2 a day and more than half (54%) live in extreme poverty earning less than US$1 a day
- 80 out of 1,000 Haitian children never see their first birthday. In the US it's 6 out of 1000
- Almost 50% of the population is unable to read or write, as compared to only 12% illiteracy in the rest of Latin America and 1% in the US
- In 2012, Haiti ranked 161st out of 187 countries in terms of human development by the United Nations Development Program.

I just finished my fourth trip there but the first time was in January 2013. There were about 25 of us, including my wife and two daughters. We did what you usually do on a Soles4Souls trip, distributed shoes to people in need, especially children. It's hard, hot and rewarding work.

We were coming back on a Saturday night to the community center where we were staying. With plumbing that mostly didn't function and food right at the borderline of acceptable, we still realized how fortunate we were compared to those around us in the small, rural community outside Port Au Prince.

Because less than 25% of Haiti is electrified, we were driving through mostly dark streets, punctuated by islands of light.

Where there weren't electric lights, many people had fires or candles. But in the pools of darkness between electric and flame, there were lots of people. They weren't just hanging out, however. They were working. Hard. When I asked our guide about it, her answer was pretty stark, "You don't sell, you don't eat." These people were still out there, in some cases you'd literally have to trip over them to find them, because they hadn't made enough money to get through the next day or two. Whether it was selling vegetables, cutting hair, repairing tires or purveying shoes, every small business owner was still getting after it. So my stereotype going in (50% unemployment must mean that they're lazy, right?) was shattered. This was not a work ethic problem. There had to be something else.

That's because it turns out Haiti is, actually, a country of entrepreneurs! The same forces that matter in the US: competition, pricing, quality, supply chain management, merchandising are just as valid in St Louis Nord as they are in St. Louis MO. And with more than 70% of the economy in the "informal sector" entrepreneurship is the only way to make a living.

As powerful as the negative statistics above are, it's only one way to understand Haiti. The numbers are abstract and that makes it hard to see the people behind the math. For me, a concrete example helps understand what's possible and no example is better than that of Marie Ange.

Marie Ange was born in Jacmel, in the south of Haiti, about 40 years ago, though she's not totally sure of her age. Her life followed the typical pattern of the time: Growing up she rarely had enough to eat...one meal a day was (and still is!) the norm. Sometimes she got electricity for part of the day. She had practically no access to clean water. You can forget about anything resembling the sanitation we're used to because in Haiti people are still dying from cholera on a regular basis. And I'm not even going to get into the incredible impact of natural disasters that regularly wiped out what little she and her family had.

Pregnant at 16 she had already quit school when she moved in with the father of her child but did not get married. 15 years later, her "husband" threw her out. That also meant her daughter, who had just had a baby at age 16, would also be on the street. Marie Ange managed to find a small shack but because she could hardly make ends meet, she was about to be evicted even from that.

So, responsible for her daughter and a malnourished grandbaby, she needed a job immediately. By luck, because there just aren't that many jobs to be had, she got a job as a cook at the Haitian American Caucus (HAC). HAC is a school and microcredit organization in Haiti and our local partner. While at HAC, Marie Ange looked around for ways to make a better living. She saw the women coming in for loans and that got her thinking. So, like a smart entrepreneur, she kept her job as a cook and opened a little market stall selling used clothes and shoes, usually going to the market early in the morning to get her daughter set up at the stall, went back to cook, then back to the market at the end of the day.

Not long after she started her micro business, she took a small loan of just $25 to buy more inventory. She went to business classes. She paid back those small loans and borrowed more to have a bigger selection. Now, two years later, she has employees and has started to sell to other vendors in the market. Recently, she bought some land and built a house. For a woman in Haiti, owning property is still rare and she has a level of security that she couldn't imagine even three years ago. Through her hard work, access to capital, training and community support, Maria Ange is actually living the dream. These days she comes to HAC to cook only when she wants to see old friends! Her pride in her accomplishment is obvious. She seems happy.

Which leads me back to Dr. Brooks and his thoughts on happiness. I'm skeptical whenever I see anything about "the secret to." Given how long we've been on this planet I'm not sure that there are that many secrets left that don't involve massive amounts of money and incredible scientific effort. Questions like "what's the secret to happiness?" might help sell books or get lots of online views but I doubt the answers are news. Just like dieting secrets mostly boil down to "eat less, eat better and exercise more," the secret to happiness is also pretty simple. To paraphrase Ronald Reagan, it might be simple but that doesn't mean it's easy.

I'm a runner, specifically an ultra runner. Ultra marathons are runs longer than a marathon, usually 50k, 50 mile, 100k or 100 mile events. Doing this for the last 10+ years has brought me immeasurable joy, friendship as well as a way to regularly test my physical, emotional, mental and spiritual limits. It also gives me plenty of time to think, to make connections and to ponder my place in the universe. Because that's the way it seems to work, I never know when or where I'll get that opportunity to make those connections real.

I was in New York City recently and went out for a run the morning after a blizzard. It had been the real deal with about 10 inches of snow, whipping wind and the miserable big city slush that they don't seem to mention when talking about how great NYC is! The wind chill was in the single digits and in no time, my feet were wet and numb and I realized that all those ads I usually ignore for running shoes with Gore-Tex actually do have a purpose. All I wanted to do was finish the run, take a hot shower and a sit down with a warm breakfast. But as I headed back to the hotel, I noticed a set of wobbly tracks in the snow. After wondering who was out in this terrible weather with a bicycle, I finally figured out they were from a grocery cart. Pretty soon I caught up with the homeless man pushing it through the icy mess. That explained why the tracks were so unstable – carts aren't designed for that weather, especially when they're filled to the brim with someone's personal belongings. This man was wearing at least four coats, along with a makeshift hat. With his head down from the effort, he was the very picture of slogging. I ran a few steps past him when it hit me right in the gut. It was guaranteed that this man's feet were immeasurably colder than mine (I was pretty sure he had spent the night outside) and he most likely didn't have the hot shower and breakfast that awaited me at my hotel. I turned back around and gave him the $10 I had stuck in pocket to buy breakfast. I don't think he could have been more surprised if I had sprouted wings and floated past him. He hadn't asked for anything and therefore didn't expect anything from the anonymous man running past him. The spark in his eyes and the gratefulness that suffused his voice when he said, "Thank you brother," were the most genuine responses I've experienced in a long time. The rest of my frigid run suddenly didn't seem all that difficult.

As awesome as the moment was, and I'm using that word in its original sense rather than the worn out one we hear so often now, it was also complicated. I mean, it's pretty obvious why he was grateful. He had to be better off for my giving him $10, right? Maybe he was just happy that someone had noticed him at all. I was mostly grateful for what I did have and, though I fight it like the devil, feeling good about doing a virtuous thing. But wasn't that in and of itself a problem? See? Pretty soon I'm chasing my tail, philosophically, and all I really wanted was to help make sure the guy could get someplace warm and maybe some hot food.

And still the question of happiness and gratitude occupies a lot of my thinking time. I'm a big fan of TED talks and listen regularly to TED Radio Hour on NPR. It's a great way to pass the time on a long run and not long ago I listened to one of their programs called Simply Happy. The idea was to explore what it means to be happy, what makes us happy and how we actually find happiness. I highly recommend listening to the entire hour but it really got me thinking about the connection between gratitude and happiness.

One of the questions I really dug into is about being grateful...does gratitude come from happiness or does happiness come from gratitude?

A Benedictine monk, Brother David Steindl-Rast, is featured in the NPR segment and he's pretty sure that gratefulness is the precursor to happiness, not the other way around. Gratitude is grounded in the practice of being in the moment, that fully appreciating the present means that we can all be happy. For me, this seems to be a reasonable explanation for the happiness I felt in India, for example, when I was surrounded for the first time by profound poverty. Yet the people I met, young and old, seemed to be content in a way that didn't make sense to me. I was 19 at the time and had grown up in the comfort of a stable, middle class family. How could someone barely making enough to put food on the table be happy? Then I heard about the "bathing scheme" where I was staying. I got a bucket of hot water every third day for a shower and that was a luxury by local standards. Even then I recognized that when I got that precious, heated water something was different. I paid total attention to the feeling of pouring it over my head. I was absolutely conscious of the order in which I did things so as to maximize the water, and the feeling, so I could make it last. I was really grateful for the pleasure of that moment and that made me very happy.

As with so many lessons, that one was mostly wasted on my younger self. But it turns out, that feeling of being "lost in the moment" is actually a key to happiness. And if Brother David comes at it from a spiritual perspective, Dr. Matt Killingworth comes at it as a scientist. Based on solid research involving tens of thousands of people in 80 countries, a wide range of income and education levels and gender balanced, people are happiest when they are in the moment. The less our minds wander, the more likely we are to be happy. Because when we're thinking about something other than what we're doing right now (and writing is a great opportunity for my mind to wander!), it turns out that way more of the time than not, we're thinking about something that makes us unhappy or causes us stress. And not just a little bit but his research says that on average our attention is somewhere else almost one third of the time! Think about that. We have this amazing supercomputer in our head. More powerful than any device ever built. We can envision ideal worlds. We can play out multiple scenarios to an endless number of problems. And yet if we're not paying attention, we mostly go to the dark side. And that turns out to be true whether we are commuting (most hated task for most of us) or exercising (guilty as charged) or just mindlessly brushing our teeth. Except for sex, during which 10% of people admitted to letting their minds wander, we spend an incredible amount of time letting unhappiness happen to us. That seems crazy but it's also totally within our power to come back to the moment because the same brain that allows us to go off on a tangent can also be our ally in focusing on matters at hand and getting back to the basic human business of increasing happiness.

I have to confess that wrestling with this topic seems more than a little indulgent. If you think about life on the globe until maybe 500 years ago, most of our energy was focused on simple survival. Whether it was wild animals, not enough food or minor illnesses, nearly everything in our natural environment was a threat. Sure Aristotle was talking about beauty and truth 2500 years ago but most of the planet was consumed with just waking up the next day. To quote Thomas Hobbes, the 17th century champion of sweetness and light, "life is nasty, brutish and short."

While that seems like ancient history to me (and most anyone reading this), it is still true for billions of people living in extreme poverty (less than $1.00/day) and billions more living in food insecurity. However, those people have a right to happiness, same as I do. They especially deserve it because it's harder earned than mine. If there's any inspiration I receive because of the work I do, it comes from so many people's ability to find gratitude and happiness in ways that seem almost like superpowers to me. Yet it may be easy, and as profound, as remembering the old adage, "it all depends on how you look at it."

Dr. Dan Gilbert, from Harvard, has written a lot about happiness, including his best selling book, *Stumbling On Happiness*. What his research shows is powerful in its simplicity because it is, surprise, 100% between our ears. It's all about how we frame the situation.

One study in particular caught my attention. They measured the happiness levels of two very distinct groups: those who had just one the lottery and those who had just become paraplegic. Certainly a very stark contrast. As you would expect, the lottery winners were on top of the world and the newly disabled were pretty unhappy. Yet a year later, their happiness levels were the same. The same. Why is that? Because all of us tend to overestimate the long-term impact of any event, whether it's getting married, the impact of an election, a promotion, infidelity or a move. Based on Dr. Gilbert's research, with very few exceptions, "it if happened more than three months ago, it doesn't matter that much to your current happiness." This is intertwined with the idea of how choice affects happiness. Study after study shows that choice, after more than just a few options, actually discourages action and makes us unhappy. Yet our daily lives are filled with more and more to choose from. Whether it's six kinds of milk, hundreds of options in your new car, or the 50,000 varieties of shoes on a shopping website, what looks like progress might actually be making us miserable.

It would be a stretch, and an insult, to say that people literally living hand to mouth should be happy because they have fewer choices than we do. But it is worth thinking about the joy that comes from simple things like clean water, a slightly used book or a new pair of shoes. I know I've seen the pleasure that shoes bring as more than once I have put shoes on feet that had never had them before.

So work that matters seems to be part of the happiness formula. Being in the moment leads to gratitude, which leads to being happy. Keeping our choices and their impact in perspective is foundational to our happiness.

I cannot think of a more fitting end to this story than to show you this picture of Marie Ange. She's standing on the foundation of her new house, complete as of September 2013. As remarkable as it is that she's been successful enough to pull this off, it is equally remarkable that she owns this land and this house. Through her determination and hard work, she knows she'll never again be thrown out of her own house. Security like this is precious anywhere but especially to someone who comes from Marie Ange's background.

She's with her husband (the second and good one) and daughter. Her pride, her satisfaction of knowing that she did, indeed, change her life and the lives of her family for at least two generations, is palpable. Think about that. Three generations of people who have a real chance at getting permanently out of poverty because she had the courage to make a difference in her life. And I know from personal experience that her gratitude for the part that Soles4Souls played in making that possible is deep and abiding.

As special as Marie Ange is, and she's something else…. there are thousands of Marie Ange's in Haiti and millions around the world. They deserve a shot at happiness. You and I can help them create the opportunities for happiness and gratitude by simply taking those shoes and clothes we are finished with and find a way to give them another life, in another country, to people who are working hard to find dignity, hope and happiness.

And in the process, perhaps find some of our own.

***

SOLES4SOULS | WEARING OUT POVERTY

About the Facilitator of

A Journey of Hearts

A facilitator is an individual who helps a group with a common objective, assists, supports and encourages them in a collaborative way, to achieve a shared participation and goal by all individuals involved in a group project!

> *Love will always be a bright light,*
> *illuminating from the inside out…*
> *With Bursts of color for all to see, as it is shiny…*
> *and shared by you and me,*
> *A Gift to one another…*
> *A sign of Peace & Gratitude towards each other…*
> *Watch as it soars from shore to shore; s*
> *urrounded with Inspiration and Love for all to enjoy!*
>
> *By Tammy Bowers - CEO Inspiring Hearts LLC ©*

As I introduce our Inspiring Hearts 1st Edition collection; I am honored, and filled with pride, to provide a platform for these amazing authors who joined with me in sharing their inspirational stories with our *"A Journey of Hearts"*.

Our authors have opened their hearts to share journeys of inspiration and courage. Some will make you laugh, some will make you cry, some will make you feel joyous inside; but most importantly, you will feel the love and strength given in a collaborative way, sharing life's ups and downs and giving a positive spin on their heartfelt journey! Our intent in sharing these life experiences is to provide hope for those going through similar situations, that together our core strength can build a bridge of HOPE and spread inspiration-lending support to help so many others.

"Faith, Family & Friends" are three words that embody me. They are my foundation taught by my parents and fortunately the same values as my in-laws. I can honestly say these three words have given me courage and support to find the strength on numerous challenges, as well as encouragement to create *"Inspiring Hearts LLC"* to share from my heart to yours!

Faith has taught me that even in the worst of times, God is right there beside me whispering in my ear, "It's all going to be Okay" and to believe it no matter what the outcome.

Family is the core of me, it a love that fuels the flame inside of me, keeps me going, knowing I can lean on each of them and they on me. I have a wonderful husband *Jeff*, as well as three incredible children, *Sarah, Josh* and *Zach*, oh yeah I said it; each of them having a section of my heart!

Friends are like family to me, many know my saying once you are a friend it is a lifetime for me. I feel fortunate to have such a large beautiful bouquet of flowers; each one different and unique and each one is a beautiful bud! Like my family, I feel bless to have them, they are my gems, my treasures and for me they are always a part of my extended family!

When I became a mother, I rediscovered my creative side, becoming involved in a variety of businesses, projects and campaigns. Most of the time eager to create and make a difference, which always makes my heart sing! I have an amazing husband who by his encouragement on this book and a variety of endeavors has always inspired me to create and so I did on numerous occasions including a mother's support group called "Little Packages". We often joked there wasn't a parenting 101 book when my daughter was a born, and to have the support of other mothers was amazing, working together as we all learned from each other was so important back then.

Around 1991, shortly after my son was born, I created a children's line of clothing called "Crafted with Care". I would create the items at night then take them to expos and trade shows to sell my wares. As most parents, I became a part of the PTA, school projects, and selected "Team mom", block parties and more until our youngest who was a year old at the time became very sick. (I'll tell you the short story as you will see the correlation to some of the authors in our book. It is in our life experiences we meet by chance, but friendships last a lifetime) After numerous test, we discovered Zach had asthma, eczema, outdoor allergies and most importantly life-threatening food allergies (all nuts, as well as to eggs). With the support of other mothers in Howard County, I created and founded the first non-profit in Howard County supporting families with food allergies, called "Take a Step Food Allergy Awareness Foundation". Alongside me were two amazing mothers Jeanine Zimmer and one who to this day is my very best friend, *Drema Bonivitacola*. Both mothers had boys of the same age as Zach (3 at the time). We supported each other and began creating awareness campaigns, eager to make a difference by educating which would eventually bring awareness and protect our children. We made an impact together as a team-created change, keeping our events positive, with education, mentorship and even creating a children's book including my nephew Joel Bowers who in high school created the illustrations. We provided educational items and supported other charities, children's programs etc... Our philosophy was simple, keep our mission positive and create an environment where everyone could learn. We developed a mentorship programs "Kids talk to Kids campaign" and Symposiums for Parents and Teens, events for everyone to enjoy such as 5K Races-Family Fun days. It was our passion to develop food allergy awareness for our sons and other families. I met the amazing singer/songwriter *Ellis Woodward*, who created the first Food Allergy Song, he gave from his heart to help our campaign, and we are still friends to this day!

As years passed, I had more experiences as a Mom with the boys especially when they were both diagnosis with Dyslexia at about 10 and 13 yrs old. For both Jeff and myself, the parental light bulb went off, to begin advocating and fighting the system for them. We gather resources to make a difference for them, as any parent would do, eager to make life easier and better than our own, we would achieved and did not allow it to define us. Zach was also diagnosis with Crohns Disease during this time, so we had health and education experiences with him. We did what needed to be done (it is what you do as parents, protect them right? I am so thankful for our friend *Robyn Engle* who sent us to meet with the staff at the *Jemicy School*. It fit like a glove and was a perfect for both of them. Jemicy helped them to develop skills and strategies to be successful as they are extremely bright boys. Providing them the confidence once they graduated, they could select the University of their choosing and so they both did at *High Point University*! To empower our children, not to let anything or anyone dictate how their lives will turn out, made them stronger, built confidence, and they now know it is up to them to make the changes they need in life that is best for them no matter what the cost.

Our life experiences as a family continued when at 18 years old, just after graduation, our daughter was diagnosed with an extremely rare and incurable kidney disorder/disease called LPHS (Loin Pain Hematuria Syndrome). This has been an extremely tough journey for the entire family, and this is the story begins in my chapter of "A Journey of Hearts". My personal journey heart 2 heart experiences helped our family grow closer, as well as reevaluate what is truly important to our family!

In 2009, I was involved in a wonderful mastermind group, we lent support to one another to find what our hearts desires in business, what would make as I put it "your heart sing". It was by their support and encouragement as well as Jeff's that I created Inspiring Hearts LLC, a boutique with unique and inspiring gifts where empowerment continues as 10% goes to a charity of choice. "It's a gift that keeps giving".

Over the years, I have it was pointed out that I am a people person because I, for the most part, enjoy meeting and talking to people. I enjoy conversation, finding out what makes others tick, and many times finding out, that they are an inspiration. People have spoken to me about personal situation, shared stories, why they choose the career or charity they created. For some of them, I am amazed as I see their resilience in difficult situations. *"We are more alike than we are unlike my friends"*, says Maya Angelou. Everyone has a story; most of us may not even realize how we have impacted each other by helping one another!

Life is beyond perfect, I can say without a doubt with mountains to climb, hills and valleys, some deeper than others, some days are difficult, but personally, I choose to put a smile on my face no matter what. I choose and want to make a difference even if only for a minute before I leave this place. We all take what we learn and just try to interpret and handle it as best we can. When the days are tough I pray, sometimes several times throughout the day, and give thanks too, because for me it is a reflection of time, a resource and a foundation of me!

As Margaret Mead once said, "Never let it be said that a small group of committed individuals cannot change the world. Indeed it's the only thing that ever has." It is always amazing to me how blessed we are to find those amazing individuals that cross our path of life over the years. People are connected for a reason. As we all know there are no do over's, life is a process, lessons learned. I am so glad we have this great platform to allow these amazing voices to be heard that may not otherwise have an opportunity. So many of these individuals have taken a bad situation and created a change, strived to make a difference. Some like me are still going through a process, some you will relate to, and some I hope will strike a chord and inspire you!

Enjoy as the inspiration touches your heart, mind and spirit,
With a grateful heart, I hope you enjoy "A Journey of Hearts"!

Tammy Bowers – CEO – Inspiring Hearts LLC ©
www.inspiringhearts.net

CPSIA information can be obtained
at www.ICGtesting.com
Printed in the USA
FFOW03n1119280415
12974FF

9 781457 532733